Thomas E. Zell

Guide to New York

Its public buildings, places of amusement, churches, hotels, &c. with a map of the city, and numerous illustrations. Together with a guide to the principal first-class stores. Also, a guide to the Hudson River, with map, Vol. 2

Thomas E. Zell

Guide to New York
Its public buildings, places of amusement, churches, hotels, &c. with a map of the city, and numerous illustrations. Together with a guide to the principal first-class stores. Also, a guide to the Hudson River, with map, Vol. 2

ISBN/EAN: 9783337377397

Printed in Europe, USA, Canada, Australia, Japan

Cover: Foto ©Lupo / pixelio.de

More available books at **www.hansebooks.com**

GUIDE

TO

NEW YORK:

ITS

𝔓ublic 𝔅uildings, 𝔓laces of 𝔄musement, 𝔊hurches, 𝔊otels, &c.

WITH A

MAP OF THE CITY,

AND NUMEROUS ILLUSTRATIONS.

TOGETHER WITH

A GUIDE TO THE PRINCIPAL FIRST-CLASS STORES
IN THE VARIOUS LINES OF TRADE.

ALSO,

A GUIDE TO THE HUDSON RIVER, (WITH MAP,)
SARATOGA AND LAKE GEORGE.

NEW YORK:

T. ELLWOOD ZELL & CO.,

No. 37 PARK ROW.

1868.

TO THE READER.

SOME may think it entirely unnecessary to make any remarks by way of introduction to a work of this nature; but when the multitude of Guide-Books, Hand-Books, and Directories is considered, we feel justified in simply stating the "wherefore" which calls this work into existence. To the descriptions of New York and vicinity which have already been published, it has been justly objected that they contain mere descriptions of buildings, etc., which fail to arrest the attention or impart that information which books of this character are expected to afford. To remedy these and other objections, this work has been compiled with great care, as to noting every object of interest in and about New York, giving "correct information" in detail, and combining, what seems to be a great want, "business with pleasure." To strangers, therefore, visiting New York, this work is intended as a correct guide to all places of interest and amusement; also as a guide to ladies and gentlemen in the purchase of goods. They will find the location of almost every kind of business in the advertising pages; and the stores there indicated are of the most reliable character, as we have allowed only those of the best standing to use our work as an advertising medium.

We have also thought it proper to incorporate in this work a Guide to the Hudson River, Saratoga, and Lake George, which we feel assured will prove of interest to the citizen and stranger.

We also wish it distinctly understood that the Compiler has not hesitated to gather the materials for this work wherever he could find them, availing himself in the freest manner, not only of the researches of others, but even of their very language, whenever it happened to suit his purpose.

CONTENTS.

Academy of Design
Astor Library
Battery
Blackwell's Island
Bible House
Bellevue Hospital
Banks
Cemeteries
Central Park
City Hall Park
City Hall
Custom House
Columbia College
College of Physicians
    " St. Francis Xavier
    " City of New York
Cooper Institute
Colored Home
    " Orphans' Asylum
Children's Aid Society
Churches
Ferry Boats
Five Points House of Industry
    "   " Mission House

Forts and Fortifications
Greenwood Cemetery
Gramercy Park
General Theological Seminary
Hack Fares
Hall of Records
Hudson River
Hotels
Home for the Friendless
High Bridge
Howard Mission
Hebrew Orphan School
Insane Asylum
Institution for Deaf and Dumb
" for Blind
Juvenile Asylum
Jews' Hospital
Leak and Watts' Orphan Asylum
Libraries
Location of Piers
Magdalen Asylums
Madison Square
Monuments
Markets
Merchants' Exchange
Mercantile Library
Newspapers
New York Historical Society
" Orphan Asylum
" University
New York Hospital

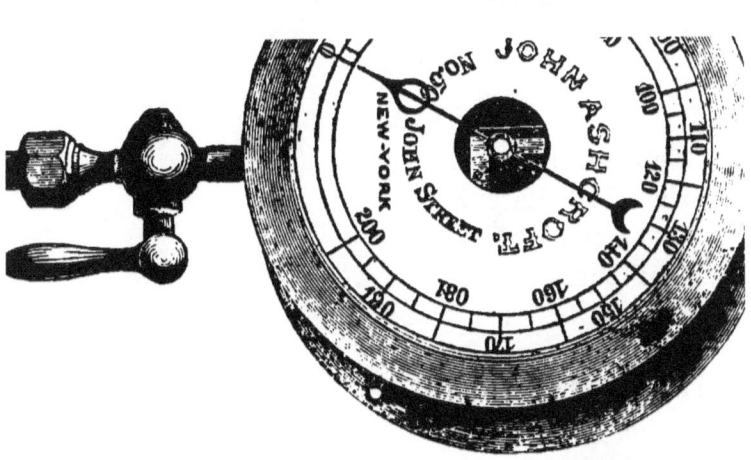

ASHCROFT'S
Steam and Water
GAUGES,
WROUGHT-IRON PIPE
FOR
Steam, Gas, and Water,
BRASS COCKS AND VALVES,
Lap-welded Boiler Flues,

And every variety of Railway and Engineers' Supplies.

JOHN ASHCROFT,
50 and 52 John Street,
NEW YORK

☞ *See page 144.*

New Court House.
New Post Office.
Odd Fellows' Hall
Omnibuses
Parks
Post Office
Places of Amusement
Police Stations
Randall's Island
Religious and Miscellaneous Institutions
Roman Catholic Orphan Asylum
Railroads
" (City)
Railroad Distances
St. Luke's Hospital
Steamboats
Squares
St. John's Park
Table of Distances
Telegraph Offices
Theatres
Tombs
Tour of the Hudson.
Union Theological Seminary
University Medical School
United States Treasury
Ward's Island
Widow's Asylum
Ward Schools
Washington Square
Watering Places

BUSINESS INDEX.

BANKERS.
Hatch, Foote & Co., (*Government Securities*)...	77
Geo. D. Arthur & Co., (*Specie*)	88
John Munroe & Co., (*Travelers' Credit*)	141

BRASS AND ZINC PLATES.
W. T. & J. Mersereau	153

BILLIARD TABLES.
Kavanagh & Decker	100

BOOKS.
A. S. Barnes & Co	28
Ivison, Phinney, Blakeman & Co	21

CARPETS.
A. Hill & Co	69
Pratt & Seymour	88

CLOTHING.
Traphagen & Hunter	46
Hyatt, Hagerman & Co	85
Freeman & Burr...........4, 20, 31, 37, 57, 103,	115

CLOTHIERS' AND TAILORS' TRIMMINGS.
Merrill & Co	121
P. A. Dailey & Co	135

CLOAKINGS.
C. H. Griffin & Co	79

CLOTHS AND CASSIMERES.
Halsted & Stiles	22
C. H. Griffin & Co	79
P. A. Dailey & Co	135

CORRUGATED IRON BUILDINGS.
Mosley's 65, 93

CURTAINS AND UPHOLSTERY.
I. E. Walraven 5

DRESS AND MANTILLA TRIMMINGS.
W. H. Elder 154

DRUGS AND MEDICINES.
Tarrant & Co. 5

DRY GOODS.
Lord & Taylor 161

FANCY GOODS AND NOTIONS.
Hastings, Potter & Co. 66
N. W. Burtis & Co. 75
Lyon Bros. 3

FANCY BASKETS.
Baums & Kahn 84

FIRE-EXTINGUISHERS.
United Fire-Extinguisher Co. 2

FISH AND PROVISIONS.
Geo. C. Parker & Bro. 132

GROCERS (Wholesale).
Fitts & Austin 124
H. Welsh 57
J. T. Wilson 41

GROCERS (Wholesale and Retail)
T. R. Agnew 22

GENTS' FURNISHING GOODS.
R. Green 138
Fisk, Clark & Flagg 108, 122

GAS WORKS.
Richter & Austin 21

HOSIERY.
Lyon Bros.. 3

HATS AND CAPS (Wholesale).
H. J. Cipperly.. 147

HOOP SKIRTS.
G. W. Lockwood & Co................................ 71

INSURANCE COMPANIES.
Home (Fire) 110
Beekman (Fire)... 112
Atlantic Mutual (Marine)....................... 34
Pacific   ("   )....................... 81

IRON WORKS.
Novelty Works.. 41
J. B. & W. W. Cornell................................ 98
Chase & Co... 127

JEWELERS.
C. A. Stevens & Co..................................... 32
Ball, Black & Co...................................... 160

LIGHTNING RODS.
J. D. West.. 19

LIQUORS.
I. Lyon... 27

LOOKING-GLASSES.
Conant Bros... 84

LIFE INSURANCE COMPANIES.
North America... 21
Brooklyn... 48
Home... 8
Berkshire... 107
Continental... 104

MACHINERY.
John Ashcroft......................................11, 144

MEERSCHAUM GOODS.

A. Ruth..	22
J. Hamburger & Co.....................................	107

MILLINERY GOODS.

B. F. Beekman & Co...................................	61
A. H. Rosenheim..	61

MUSIC PUBLISHERS.

C. H. Ditson & Co......................................	64
Horace Waters...	157

MUSICAL INSTRUMENTS.

J. Howard Foote...	62

NEWSPAPERS.

Phrenological Journal and Life Illustrated..	53

OPTICIANS.

J. H. Semmons...	150

ORGANS.

Philip Phillips & Co..................................	30
Horace Waters...	157

PIANOS.

Horace Waters...	157

POCKET-BOOKS.

Bardwell & Hopkins....................................	61

PROVISIONS.

J. Wheaton & Co..	27

PUMPS.

J. D. West...	19

RAILWAY AND ENGINEERS' SUPPLIES.

John Ashcroft...	11, 144

SAFES.

Wilders'..	84

SCALES.
Fairbanks & Co.................................... 25

STATIONERY.
Francis & Loutrell............................... 42

SEWING-MACHINES.
Chase & Co.. 131

SEWING SILKS.
Belding Bros. & Co............................... 3

SADDLERY.
Rothhan & Co..................................... 90

SILVER-PLATED WARE.
Adams, Price & Co................................ 54
Hall, Elton & Co................................. 88

TOYS.
Dennison & Co.................................... 58

TOYS (Wholesale).
R. Foulds... 28
American Toy Co................................... 6
C. F. A. Hinrichs................................. 116

TOYS (Retail).
S. J. Parsells.................................... 27

TRUST COMPANIES.
United States Trust Co............................ 44
National   "   " 38

TURKISH BATHS.
Miller, Wood & Co................................ 50

WATCHES AND FANCY GOODS.
Ve. J. Magnin, Guédin & Co....................... 128

WOODEN AND WILLOW WARE.
J. S. Barron & Co................................ 94
M. & G. Wilkinson................................ 107

2*

NEW YORK.

The Island of Manhattan was discovered by Henry Hudson in 1609, and settled by immigrants from Holland in 1614. The West India Company in 1626 purchased the entire island, containing 22,000 acres, from the Indians, for sixty guilders, or twenty-four dollars. From its earliest period, the then called "Nieuw Amsterdam" had a varied history. The English regarded it as a valuable acquisition, and took it from the Dutch in 1664, who succeeded, however, in recovering it in 1676. About one year thereafter it was ceded again to the British, and received the name of New York, in honor of James, Duke of York. In 1666 the city contained two hundred houses and about one thousand inhabitants. From that early period to the present it has made great progress in buildings, population, and governmental arrangements.

The present population of the city is about one million. New York is the largest and most wealthy city on this Continent. Its commercial relations extend to the "uttermost parts of the earth."

The length of the city from the southern to the

WEST'S IMPROVED PUMP,

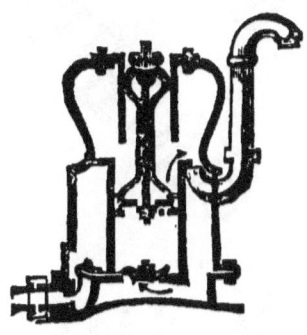

ANTI-FREEZING AND DOUBLE-ACTING.

THE BEST IN USE.

"We do know that the West Pump is all that any man ever requires, being economical, desirable, and efficient."— *N. Y. Tribune.*

SANCHO-PANZA WIND-MILL,

SELF-REGULATING, SELF-ADJUSTING, and SELF-OILING.

THE LATEST AND BEST.

"It is very strongly built, is cheap, and always under perfect control."— *Scientific American.*

OTIS'
PATENT LIGHTNING-RODS,

Of Copper or Galvanized Iron. The only perfect insulation in America.

The rod supported outside of the glass, and not in contact with it, and not even a water-connection with the building when it rains.

"I would recommend to the public the use of the Otis' Patent Lightning Conductors."—*Hon. Horace Mann.*

☞ Agents wanted everywhere, with exclusive right.

J. D. WEST & CO.,
No. 40 Courtlandt St., New York.

FREEMAN & BURR, CLOTHIERS

Merchant Tailors

AND

OUTFITTERS,

IN

Gentlemen's & Boys' Clothing

OF EVERY DESCRIPTION.

FURNISHING GOODS, &c.

THE
BEST FOREIGN & DOMESTIC FABRICS,
Always in Stock for Orders and to Measure.

FREEMAN & BURR,

No. 124 FULTON ST., and 90 NASSAU ST.,

(S. E. Corner Fulton and Nassau Sts.,)

NEW YORK.

229 BROADWAY,
Corner of Barclay Street.

N. D. MORGAN, President.

POLICIES SECURED BY SPECIAL PLEDGE OF PUBLIC STOCKS

in the Insurance Department of the State of New York, and each REGISTERED POLICY will bear a CERTIFICATE to that effect, countersigned by the SUPERINTENDENT of the INSURANCE DEPART.

    This feature of security originated with this Company and was the invention of its present President. Nearly **FIVE MILLIONS** of its policies are already secured in this manner. Communications addressed to the principal office, or to any of its agencies, will be promptly attended to.

J. W. MERRILL, Secretary.

NEW YORK & HARBOR.

IVISON, PHINNEY, BLAKEMAN & CO.,
PUBLISHERS OF THE
AMERICAN EDUCATIONAL SERIES
OF
SCHOOL BOOKS,
AND
GENERAL WHOLESALE DEALERS IN
BOOKS AND STATIONERY,
47 and 49 GREENE STREET,
(Between Grand and Broome Streets,)
New York.

☞ Over four million books of the above series sold annually.

HENRY IVISON. AUG. C. TAYLOR.
HENRY F. PHINNEY. DAVID B. IVISON.
BIRDSEY BLAKEMAN.

GAS-WORKS,

For Towns, Factories, Hotels, Country Dwellings, etc.

HIRZEL'S GERMAN APPARATUS (*not Gasoline*).

The Gas produced by this apparatus possesses five times the illuminating power of Coal Gas; hence, to do the same service, Works of only *one-fifth* the capacity are needed, thus saving in space and capital invested. Cost of Gas, from one-half to one-fifth that of Coal Gas.

These Works are in successful operation in *Europe and America;* among others, the extensive Brass Works of Holmes, Booth & Haydens, Waterbury, Conn., are lighted.

Circular with Certificates, on application to the Manufacturers,

RICHTER & AUSTIN,
Office, 2 *Hanover Buildings,*
New York.

Cloth House.

HALSTED & STILES,

43 and 45 White Street, New York,

IMPORTERS AND JOBBERS OF

Fancy Cassimeres, Doeskins, Cloths, Coatings and Vestings.

Merchant Tailors, Clothiers, and other Dealers, whether buying in large or small quantities, are invited to make our acquaintance.

---

415   A. RUTH,   415

Meerschaum Manufactory,

415 Broome Street, 415

near Broadway.

PIPES MADE TO ORDER.

ALSO,

AMBERS,

AND ALL KINDS OF REPAIRING.

415   **BROOME ST.**   415

THOS. R. AGNEW,

IMPORTER AND DEALER IN

FINE GROCERIES, CHOICE TEAS, &c.

260 and 262 Greenwich Street, cor. of Murray,

NEW YORK.

northern portion is twelve miles, with an average width of two miles. The streets and avenues above Fourteenth street run at right angles. A fine view of New York and vicinity may be had from Trinity Church steeple.

New York possesses very many buildings, both public and private, of rare beauty and elegance, together with the parks, places of amusement, churches, hotels, &c., to which we hasten to invite attention.

CENTRAL PARK.

There is probably no place on the Island of Manhattan of equal interest to the stranger or citizen with Central Park. In 1858 work was commenced on it, and in about one year it was thrown open to the public. Up to the present time, ten million dollars have been expended upon it. It contains eight hundred and fifty acres, is two and a half miles long, and half a mile wide : extending from Fifty-ninth to One Hundred and Tenth street, and from Fifth to Eighth avenue. It is, with three exceptions, the largest park in the world. It has over nine miles of carriage-drive and twenty-five miles of walk. Three hundred and ten thousand trees and shrubs have been planted, and workmen are constantly employed in improving and planting flowers, shrubbery, &c. There are about thirty-four archways and bridges of great variety and exquisite beauty, no two being alike. The Terrace is the leading architectural structure. This is at the end of the Mall on the north. Below it is the Esplanade, with a beautiful fountain in the centre. There is so much beauty in the Park, and in such great variety, that it is impossible within the limits of this work to mention it in detail It possesses all that is picturesque,—lake, stream, hill, valley, rock, plain and slope. During the skating season great numbers frequent the Park, as the lakes are free to all. When the ice is in good condition, a red ball is hoisted on the Arsenal building, (within the Park,) and the city cars, running to the Park, indicate by small flags when the skating is good.

At the gates of the Park are to be found carriages for hire. Not being under the control of the Park Commissioners, they are not responsible for their regulation or charges. The great attractions of the Park are only to be seen by taking the foot-paths. Throughout the Park are to be found the police, dressed in gray suits, who are required to give any information about the Park to visitors, and to preserve order.

The Park may be reached by the Sixth, Seventh and Eighth avenue cars, also by the Central Park, North and East River Railroads, either division, up West or South streets. None of the stages run within *seventeen* blocks of the Park. The above are the *only* lines of cars that run to the Park gates. Some other lines advertise to run there, whereas they do not run within a half a mile of it.

THE BATTERY.

This once beautiful promenade of the fashion and *elite* of New York has been converted into a landing place for immigrants and the rendezvous for immigrant runners, thieves, pickpockets and ruffians of "the baser sort." Originally it was a delightful retreat in the summer time for pleasure seekers, who sought the fresh sea-air under the shade of its stately trees. Connected with it is Castle Garden, originally a fortification, but now used by the Commissioner of Emigration. The beauty and glory of both have departed.

CITY HALL PARK.

This also has lost its attractions. Within its enclosure is the City Hall, Hall of Records, *New* Court House, Rotunda, *Old* Court House, Fountain and statue of what is intended to represent De Witt Clinton. It is supposed that a new Post Office building will be erected on the southern portion of this Park.

ST. JOHN'S PARK

Is located between Laight, Varick and Hudson streets. Private property.

WASHINGTON SQUARE.

This was once occupied as the "Potter's Field." It contains about ten acres, and is beautifully

* Recently sold for $1,000,000, and a freight depot erected thereon by the Hudson Railroad Company.

decorated with shrubbery, and a fountain in the centre. Situated been Fourth and Eighth streets, two blocks west of Broadway.

UNION PARK

Is on Broadway and Fourth avenue, between Fourteenth and Seventeenth streets. This Park has also a fountain. Near here is the equestrian statue of Washington.

GRAMERCY PARK.

Located between Twentieth and Twenty-first treets, and Third and Fourth avenues. Private property.

STUYVESANT PARK

Extends from Fifteenth to Seventeenth street, and is divided by the Second avenue.

TOMPKINS SQUARE

Occupies an area formed by Avenues A and B, and Seventh and Tenth streets.

MADISON SQUARE.

This Park contains ten acres; is at the junction of Broadway and Fifth avenue. Near the Square stands the monument of General Worth.

FRENCH, GERMAN & SWISS TOYS.

S. J. PARSELLS,
36 JOHN STREET, NEW YORK,

IMPORTER AND DEALER IN

The Finest Assortment of Wax Dolls in the City.

Building, Alphabet, and Mosaic Blocks.

J. WHEATON & CO.
Commission Merchants

AND DEALERS IN

Provisions and Groceries,

261 WASHINGTON STREET,

JOHN WHEATON.
GEO. P. DODD.
C. G. ENDICOTT.
} NEW YORK.

I. LYON,
IMPORTER OF AND DEALER IN

GROCERIES, LIQUORS, CIGARS,
AND
SHIP STORES,
164 Greenwich Street,
(Corner Courtlandt Street,)

New York.

Great Improvement in Writing-Pens.

This celebrated Patent is constructed upon purely scientific principles involved in the use of *two lateral arches or corrugations upon the back*, acting in opposition to the usual forward arch or bowl of the pen, ensuring *a perfect pen* in the important particulars of *strength, elasticity, evenness of point, and smoothness of execution.*

These pens are sold by all stationers, or may be procured of the Manufacturers by mail, prepaid, on receipt of price, as follows:

One dozen SCIENTIFIC PENS (assorted points) and INK-RETAINING PEN-HOLDER, 50 cents.

SCIENTIFIC GOLD PEN ($3) with INK-RETAINING HOLDER, $4.50.

A GOLD PEN is *given away* to the purchaser of each 12th gross (or fraction of 12th gross) of STEEL PENS, bought of a retail stationer.

Orders from the trade solicited. Liberal terms to agents.

A. S. BARNES & CO.,
Wholesale Booksellers and Stationers,
111 and 113 William Street, New York.

ROBERT FOULDS,

IMPORTER OF

FANCY GOODS, CHINA,

AND

FIREWORKS,

No. 39 John Street,

New York.

CITY HALL.

This is a very fine edifice, of the Corinthian order of architecture, with a marble front, and sides and rear of sandstone. Erected between the years 1803 and 1810. In the building are the several offices of the Mayor, Aldermen, and Common Council rooms, Governor's rooms, containing portraits of Governors of the State and Mayors of the City. Open daily.

CUSTOM HOUSE.

This building was formerly the Merchants' Exchange. Is located on the square bounded by Wall and Exchange Place and William and Hanover streets. The material is of Quincy granite. Front on Wall street two hundred feet, with a depth of one hundred and seventy-one feet. The portico, of eighteen Ionic columns, imparts to it an imposing effect. Erected in 1836, at a cost of two million dollars.

UNITED STATES TREASURY,

Corner of Wall and Nassau streets, is a beautiful building, of the Doric order of Grecian architecture, in imitation of the celebrated Pantheon at Athens. Fronting on Wall street there are eight Grecian columns, thirty-two feet high, with a corresponding number on Pine street. Cost of the building and grounds, $1,200,000.

NEW COURT HOUSE.

This immense building, now in process of construction, is situated in the rear of the City Hall, on Chamber street, and will be, when completed, one of the most substantial edifices in the United States. It was commenced in the fall of 1861, but it is impossible to determine when it will be finished. The entire length of the building is two hundred and fifty feet, and the breadth one hundred and fifty; rectangular in form, and three stories in height, above ground. From the base course to the top of pediment, is ninety-seven feet. The dome will be one hundred and twenty-eight feet high, above the pediment; making a total height of the building, from the base course to the top of the dome, two hundred and twenty-five feet.

The original cost was estimated at about $2,000,000, but, thus far, over $3,000,000 have been expended upon it.

It is constructed of marble and iron, and is an entirely fire-proof building.

The court-rooms are large, airy, and unobstructed by columns, made with reference to the principles of acoustics, and finished in an agreeable and pleasing manner; so that they form an attractive feature to the spectator, and all to whom may be intrusted the administration of justice.

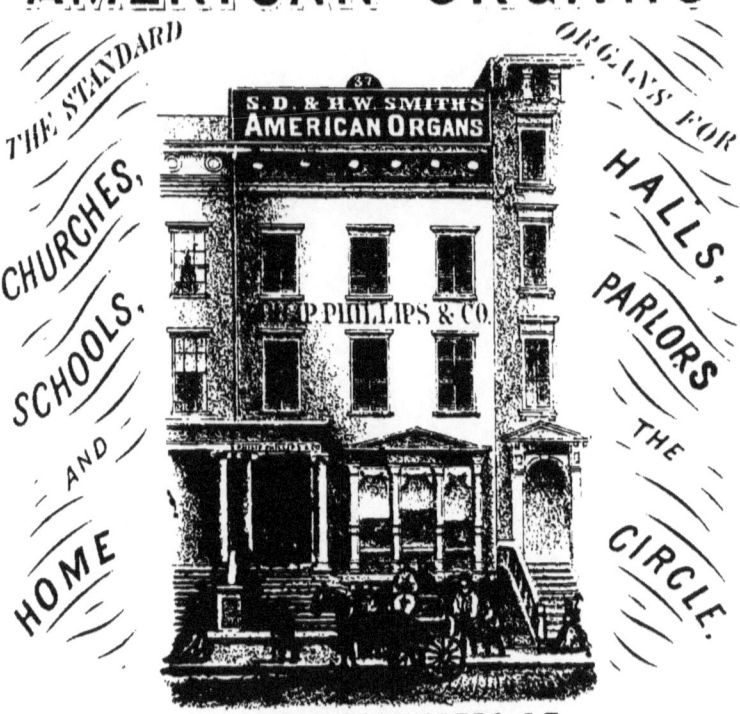

FREEMAN & BURR, CLOTHIERS

Merchant Tailors

AND

OUTFITTERS,

IN

Gentlemen's & Boys' Clothing

OF EVERY DESCRIPTION.

FURNISHING GOODS, &c.

THE
BEST FOREIGN & DOMESTIC FABRICS,
Always in Stock for Orders and to Measure.

FREEMAN & BURR,

No. 124 FULTON ST., and 90 NASSAU ST.,

(S. E. Corner Fulton and Nassau Sts.,)

NEW YORK.

C. A. STEVENS & CO.

Gold & Silversmiths,

IMPORTERS OF

WATCHES,

DIAMONDS, CLOCKS,

BRONZES and FANCY GOODS,

MANUFACTURERS OF

FINE JEWELRY.

Particular attention given to the Manufacture of SILVER WARE for Presentation and Weddings. Also, to the Setting of Diamonds and other Gems.

40 EAST 14th STREET,
(UNION SQUARE,)

NEW YORK.

THE NEW POST OFFICE.

A plan for this building has at last been decided upon, and it will be put up under the superintendence of five architects, at a cost of $3,500,000. The work will commence as soon as Congress makes the appropriation. The building will cover the whole plot of ground, and made of granite, marble, and iron. The style of architecture is the pure French Renaissance. It will be three stories high, surmounted by a Mansard roof, marked by a centre pavilion four stories high. The pavilion in front will be 160 feet high, and the building facing the City Hall will be 320 feet in length. The first story will be 22 feet high, composed of arched openings, supported upon square piers; the second will be 18 feet high, and the third 16. The style of the building is that of the Tuileries and the Hotel de Ville. The building will display the following statues: America, Commerce, Industry, Washington, Franklin, Justice, History, Peace, Strength, Truth, Genius of the Arts, Virtue, Honor, Literature, Mechanics, Genius of Science, Agriculture, and Navigation. The public corridor will be 25 feet wide, and 600 feet in length, entered from Broadway and Park Row. The building can be completed, it is claimed, in two years. Clocks are to be placed at various points around the building for the accommodation of the public.

NEW YORK UNIVERSITY.

This magnificent piece of architecture is located on the east side of Washington square. The edifice is of marble, and has a front of two hundred feet, with a depth of about eighty feet. The University was established in 1831, and has ever maintained a high and noble reputation.

COLUMBIA COLLEGE.

This is the oldest Institution of the kind in the city, having been established in 1754. The present structure, located on Forty-ninth street near Fifth avenue, was erected in 1855. It has a very fine library of twenty thousand volumes.

COLLEGE OF PHYSICIANS.

This Institution is located at 53 East Twenty-third street, near Fourth avenue. It was founded in 1807. Has a fine library and an anatomical museum. Visitors admitted to the museum on application at the College.

UNION THEOLOGICAL SEMINARY

Is located in University Place, between Eighth and Ninth streets. It was founded in 1836. Has accommodations for about one hundred and fifty students.

THE GENERAL THEOLOGICAL SEMINARY,

Under the management of the Episcopal Church, is situated on the corner of Twentieth street and Ninth avenue. There are two buildings of stone, capable of accommodating two hundred pupils.

COLLEGE OF ST. FRANCIS XAVIER.

This Institution is located in Fifteenth street, between Fifth and Sixth avenues. It was founded in 1850. Is under the management and direction of the Roman Catholics.

WARD SCHOOLS.

There are about two hundred and eighty of these valuable institutions in New York. Many of them have very fine buildings, that are alike an ornament and an honor to the city.

UNIVERSITY MEDICAL SCHOOL.

In Fourteenth street, between Irving place and Third avenue. This institution has a very fine library, and an extensive museum. Open to visitors from ten A. M. to six P. M.

COLLEGE OF THE CITY OF NEW YORK,

Formerly called the Free Academy, is located in Twenty-third street, corner of Lexington avenue; was established in 1848 by the Board of Education of New York, for the purpose of providing a higher education for such pupils of the common schools as pass a proper examination. It is supported entirely by the city. The building is a fine structure, in the style of the town-halls of the Netherlands, one hundred and twenty-five feet on Lexington avenue, with a depth of eighty feet on Twenty-third street. Will accommodate about one thousand pupils. Cost of building and grounds, $120,000.

NEW YORK HISTORICAL SOCIETY.

This institution is located on the corner of Second avenue and Eleventh street. Was established in 1810. Its literary collections consist of rare and valuable books pertaining to the history and antiquities of the country, together with maps, coins, medals, etc.; also, a very choice library of twenty-three thousand volumes. Open to visitors from 10 A. M. till 5 P. M.

COOPER INSTITUTE.

This splendid building, of brown stone, was erected by Mr. Peter Cooper, in the year 1857, at a cost of six hundred thousand dollars. The structure covers an entire block, having a front on Eighth street of one hundred and forty-five feet; on Seventh street, eighty-six feet; and on Third and Fourth avenues, each one hundred and ninety-five feet. Mr. Cooper presented it, when

FREEMAN & BURR, CLOTHIERS

Merchant Tailors

AND

OUTFITTERS,

IN

Gentlemen's & Boys' Clothing

OF EVERY DESCRIPTION.

FURNISHING GOODS, &C.

THE

BEST FOREIGN & DOMESTIC FABRICS,

Always in Stock for Orders and to Measure

FREEMAN & BURR,

No. 124 FULTON ST., and 90 NASSAU ST.,

(S. E. Corner Fulton and Nassau Sts.,)

NEW YORK.

NATIONAL TRUST COMPANY,

CAPITAL, $1,000,000.

Office, 336 BROADWAY.

OF THE CITY OF NEW YORK.

JAMES MERRILL, *Sec'y*.   DARIUS R. MANGAN, *Pres't*.

The NATIONAL TRUST COMPANY receives DEPOSITS in LARGE or SMALL amounts, and permits them to be drawn as a whole or in part BY CHECK AT SIGHT and WITHOUT NOTICE, allowing FOUR PER CENT. INTEREST ON ALL DAILY BALANCES, AND FIVE PER CENT. ON ALL SPECIAL deposits of six months or longer. As it also makes collections at all points at the most favorable rates, parties can keep current accounts in this institution with special advantages of SECURITY, CONVENIENCE, AND PROFIT.

COOPER UNION.

completed, as a free gift, to a Board of Trustees, for the "moral, intellectual and physical improvement of his countrymen." There is a large hall for public meetings, lectures, etc., capable of seating three thousand persons, in what may be termed the basement. Although twenty feet below the sidewalk, yet it is well lighted, and far better ventilated than any of the theatres or public halls in New York. The upper stories contain galleries for paintings and sculpture, lecture-rooms, library and free reading-room, together with rooms for the School of Design for women. Open to all, free, from 10 A. M. to 9 P. M.

THE TOMBS.

This massive stone structure, in the Egyptian style of architecture, erected in 1838, is the City Prison. Located on the square bounded by Centre, Elm, Franklin and Leonard streets; has about one hundred and seventy-five cells. In the interior court-yard is where the execution of criminals take place. Open to visitors on application at the entrance on Franklin street.

HIGH BRIDGE.

This very fine and important structure is thrown across the Harlem river, about eight miles from the City Hall. It was erected in 1842, at a cost of one million dollars. The Bridge supports the pipes conducting the Croton water to the receiving reservoir in the Central Park.

It is one thousand four hundred and fifty feet in length, and one hundred and twenty feet high from the water. The material of which this imposing object is constructed is granite, and probably there is not to be found a finer piece of masonry in the country. This splendid bridge can be reached by the Harlem steamboats, or Third avenue cars to Harlem and thence by steamboat.

THE BIBLE HOUSE.

This gigantic edifice, occupying the entire square bounded by Third and Fourth avenues and Eighth and Ninth streets, is constructed of brick, with brown stone facings. It was erected in 1853, at a cost of three hundred thousand dollars. It is the property of the American Bible Society. Since the organization of the Society in 18 , it has put in circulation about ten million Bibles and Testaments. The building is accessible to strangers at all times, and the managers take great pleasure in conducting visitors through its various departments.

BLACKWELL'S ISLAND.

There is upon this Island the Penitentiary, Alms House, Lunatic Asylum and Work House; all of them built of granite, and very spacious structures. Tickets for admission to the Island can be obtained at the Alms House Department, in the Rotunda, near the Hall of Records.

ARCHITECTURAL DEPARTMENT
OF THE
Novelty Iron Works,
77 AND 83 LIBERTY STREET,
Corner of Broadway,
New York.

Complete Fire-Proof Buildings, Corrugated Iron Roofs, Columns, Lintels, Floors, Casings, Shutters, Vaults, Safes, Railings, and all Cast and Wrought Iron Work used in and about BUILDINGS. Also, BRIDGES and IRON PIERS.

Henry J. Davison,
Wm. W. Ayres, } *Agents.*
J. Heuvelman,

HORATIO ALLEN, *President.*
W. P. TROWBRIDGE, *Vice Pres't.*
J. WILSON STRATTON, *Sec. & Treas.*

J. T. WILSON,
Wholesale Grocer,
109 & 111 Warren Street,
New York.

NO DRUMMERS EMPLOYED.

With a surplus always on hand, purchases are made for net cash only.

Customers of the house have this advantage, that they have neither to help pay drummers' expenses, nor interest on time-purchases.

BLANK BOOKS, STATIONERY, &c.

FRANCIS & LOUTREL,

45 Maiden Lane, New York,

STEAM JOB PRINTERS, LITHOGRAPHERS,

AND

BLANK BOOK MANUFACTURERS.

Account Books, Writing Papers, Fancy and Staple Stationery, every kind for business, professional, or private use, in quantities to suit,

AT LOW PRICES.

Diaries and Daily Journals,

Photograph Albums, Gold Pens, Chessmen, Pocket Cutlery, Drawing Materials and Paper, Mourning Paper and Envelopes, Portfolios, Cards, Writing Desks, Expense Books, Time Books, CROTON Inks and Fluids, Ink Trays, &c., &c.

INDELIBLE
Post-Office Stamping-Ink.

Copy your Letters. — Use Francis' Improved Manifold Letter-Writer, by which Letters and Copies are written at the same time. Copying and Seal Presses.

TO PRINTERS. — Francis & Loutrel's PATENT COMPOSITION for Inking Rollers is superior to anything in use; does not harden, shrink, or crack, and always remains moist. Can be re-cast.

Please call or send orders to

FRANCIS & LOUTREL,

STATIONERS, PRINTERS AND BOOKBINDERS,

45 Maiden Lane, New York.

WARD'S ISLAND.

Contains the Refuge and Nursery Houses and the State Emigrant Hospital. Permits to visit the Island procured from the Commissioners of Emigration, office at Castle Garden.

RANDALL'S ISLAND.

Here are the nurseries for the support and instruction of destitute children.

The elegant and massive structures which cover this famous group of islands make a striking feature in the landscape, as we sail up the East river. A very fine view of all the public buildings on these islands may be had by taking the Harlem boat at Peck Slip, East river.

POST OFFICE.

The New York Post Office is situated in Nassau, between Liberty and Cedar streets. It was formerly the Middle Dutch Church, erected in 1693. It has been used as a Post Office since 1843. The Office is opened continuously, except Sundays; then it is open from 9 to 10 A. M., and 12½ to 1½ P. M. There are six hundred Lamp Post Letter Boxes scattered throughout the city, from which letters are collected six times daily.

HALL OF RECORDS.

This rather imposing structure was formerly used as a prison. It is built of stone, stuccoed.

Located at the corner of Centre and Chatham streets. Now used for the purpose its name indicates.

MERCHANTS' EXCHANGE.

We regret to say the merchants of New York do not possess a very imposing place for meeting "on change." Their rooms are in Pine street, near Nassau. Exchange Sales Room, 110 Broadway.

ACADEMY OF DESIGN.

This splendid building is located on the corner of Twenty-third street and Third avenue, and is probably one of the most remarkable structures of the kind in the city. Erected at a cost of one hundred and fifty thousand dollars. The annual exhibitions of the Academy are held during the months of April, May, June and July, during which the building is open to the public for a small admission fee.

THE INSTITUTION FOR THE DEAF AND DUMB.

This noble Institution is on Washington Heights, near One Hundred and Fiftieth street, East river. The building has accommodations for about three hundred pupils. They are instructed in the various branches of learning, and those that desire it are taught some useful trade. Visitors admitted daily,

U.S. TRUST COMPANY OF NEW YORK,
49 WALL ST. COR. WILLIAM.
CAPITAL AND SURPLUS, $2,000,000.

This Company is a legal depository for moneys paid into Court and is authorized to act as guardian or receiver of estates.
INTEREST ALLOWED ON DEPOSITS
which may be made and withdrawn at any time, and will be entitled to interest for the whole time they may remain with the Company.

JOHN A. STEWART, President.
WILLIAM DARROW, Secretary.
WILLIAM H. MACY
JOHN J. CISCO } V. Presidents.

except Sunday, from 1 to 4 o'clock P. M. The Asylum can be reached by the Hudson River Railroad to Fanwood Station.

INSTITUTION FOR THE BLIND,

Is located on Ninth avenue, between Thirty-third and Thirty-fourth streets. The structure of granite is of the Gothic order of architecture, and surrounded by a beautiful lawn, tastefully disposed with shrubs and flowers. The building can accommodate some four hundred pupils. They are instructed in the various branches pursued in our schools of learning. Many of them are very proficient in music, and others sustain themselves by their skill in some useful handicraft. Visitors are admitted on week-days from 1 to 6 P. M. Eighth or Ninth avenue cars run to it.

FIVE POINTS HOUSE OF INDUSTRY.

This wonderful and praiseworthy institution was founded through the exertions of Rev. Mr. Pease, in 1848. It is located 155 Worth street, near Centre, what was once the very Sodom of wickedness. Mr. Pease commenced his labors here under great difficulties, but, with great perseverance, he has achieved a wonderful success. Thousands of little wanderers have been taken from the surrounding abodes of vice and poverty and provided with good homes. In 1857 Mr. Pease retired from the House of Industry to take charge of the farm connected with the Institution, in Westchester county. Visitors are always welcome. Mr. S. B. Halliday is the present Superintendent.

FIVE POINTS MISSION HOUSE,

Built on the sight of the "Old Brewery," in 1852, is a fine brick structure, four stories, well adapted for the purpose for which it was constructed. It is under the control and management of the Ladies' Home Missionary Society of the Methodist Episcopal Church. The Institution has for its aim and object the gathering in and providing homes for the children of poverty and shame, with which that neighborhood abounds. It is located immediately opposite the Five Points House of Industry. Visitors admitted daily from 9 A. M. till 5 P. M.

HOWARD MISSION AND HOME FOR LITTLE WANDERERS.

This is probably the largest establishment of the kind in the city. Located at No. 37 New Bowery; was opened in 1861, since which time nearly seven thousand children have been received. Those to be sent to homes, remain day and night in the Mission; the others enjoy the benefit of the bath, wardrobe, dining and school-rooms, but do not sleep at the Mission. About five hundred are daily at the table. The Board of Managers

Traphagen, Hunter & Co.

398, 400 & 402 BOWERY
NEW YORK.

CLOTHING

Of superior style and quality, ready made or to order, at rates full 20 per cent. below Broadway prices.

GOODS WARRANTED AS REPRESENTED, OR MONEY REFUNDED.

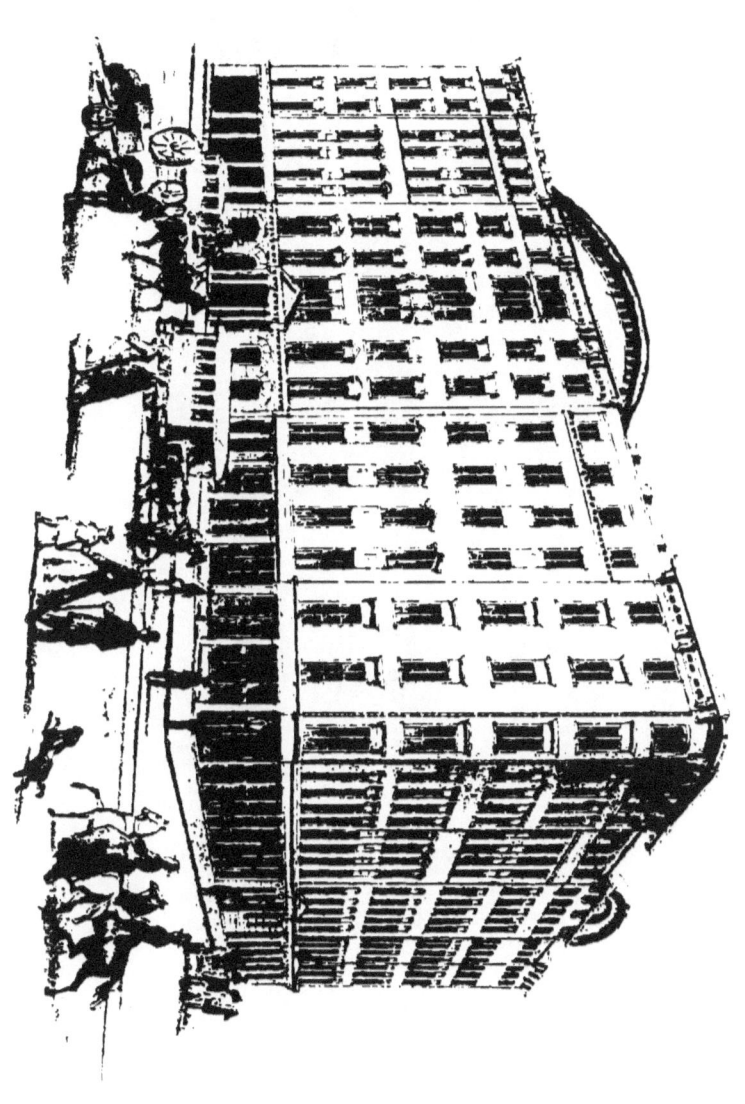

represents all the evangelical denomination of Christians. Sustained by free-will offerings. Visitors admitted on application at the Home.

CHILDREN'S AID SOCIETY.

This Society is doing a noble work in the reclamation of vagrant children. Its organization is very simple: a central office; agents to find poor children; schools to educate them and give them habits of industry; lodging houses to shelter, train and clothe them, and agents to convey them to homes in the West. It was organized in 1853, and since that time has provided homes for eleven thousand children. There are thirteen Industrial Schools connected with the Institution. The object of the Society is to teach the children various industrial pursuits, as well as to educate them.

It has under its charge the News Boys' Lodging House, at 128 Fulton street, and Girls' Lodging House, at 205 Canal street. Central office, No. 11 Clinton Hall, Astor Place.

MAGDALEN ASYLUMS.

There are three of these praiseworthy institutions in New York, located as follows: Eighty-eighth street west of Bloomingdale road; corner of Mulberry and Houston streets, and 22 West Houston street. The object of these Asylums is to provide a home for fallen women, who manifest a desire to retrace the wrong steps they have taken; and they are intended as a Home, not as a place of confinement. A Home where may be found kind looks, affectionate words, earnest entreaty and wholesome advice. A Home whose inmates, sheltered by good influences and withdrawn entirely from the scenes of dissipation, may carry out their resolves to forsake, with divine aid, the allurements of sin, and prove by their future lives the sincerity of their efforts.

LEAKE AND WATT'S ORPHAN ASYLUM

Is located on One Hundred and Seventeenth street, between Fourth and Fifth avenues. It was founded by the two individuals whose names it bears. The building is a very fine one, with about twenty-six acres of ground surrounding it; can accommodate two hundred children. Visitors admitted every afternoon. Can be reached by the Harlem cars.

WIDOWS' ASYLUM

Is located on Fourteenth street, near Second avenue. The object of the Institution is to provide a home for indigent old ladies over seventy years of age. One hundred dollars is charged as an entrance fee; then they are provided for during life without any additional expense. Open to visitors every day.

COLORED HOME,

For aged and indigent colored persons, is situated at the foot of Sixty-fifth street, East river Visitors admitted on application.

HEBREW ORPHAN SCHOOL,

Under the management of the Jews, and for the reception of poor Hebrew orphan children, is located on East Seventy-seventh street, near Third avenue. Visitors welcomed.

NEW YORK ORPHAN ASYLUM

Is situated on the Bloomingdale road, near Eightieth street. The building is one hundred and twenty feet by sixty, surrounded by ample grounds, commanding a fine view of the Hudson river. The Institution was incorporated in 1807. The present edifice was erected in 1840. Visitors admitted daily.

INSANE ASYLUM

Is also situated on the Bloomingdale road, near One Hundred and Seventeenth street. It occupies a beautiful and commanding sight, and its approaches and surroundings are admirably fitted to lighten the sense of depression and gloom so often associated with establishments of this kind. A visit to the Asylum will amply repay any one who either loves the beauties of nature, or the still greater beauties of beneficence in orderly, efficient and extensive action. Open to visitors daily.

COLORED ORPHAN ASYLUM.

This Institution formerly occupied a fine building on Fifth avenue, but it was destroyed by the mob in the riots of July, 1863. They are now located at the foot of One Hundred and Fifty-first street, North River. Strangers are always welcome.

ROMAN CATHOLIC ORPHAN ASYLUMS.

The Asylum for girls is located at the corner of Prince and Mott streets. For boys, corner of Fifth avenue and Fifty-first street.

HOME FOR THE FRIENDLESS

Is situated on East Thirtieth street, near Fifth avenue. Is for the protection of deserted children, and adult persons who are in distress.

JUVENILE ASYLUM.

This beautiful edifice is located on One Hundred and Seventy-fifth street, near Tenth avenue. The Institution occupies about twenty acres of ground, which is in part cultivated by the children, who, during their stay in the Asylum, are instructed in all the branches of a common school education. There are about seven hundred children in the Institution. The Asylum can be reached by the Hudson River Road to Fort Washington.

NEW YORK HOSPITAL.

These buildings of gray stone and grounds occupy a block between Duane and Worth streets. Entrance on Broadway. This admirable Institu-

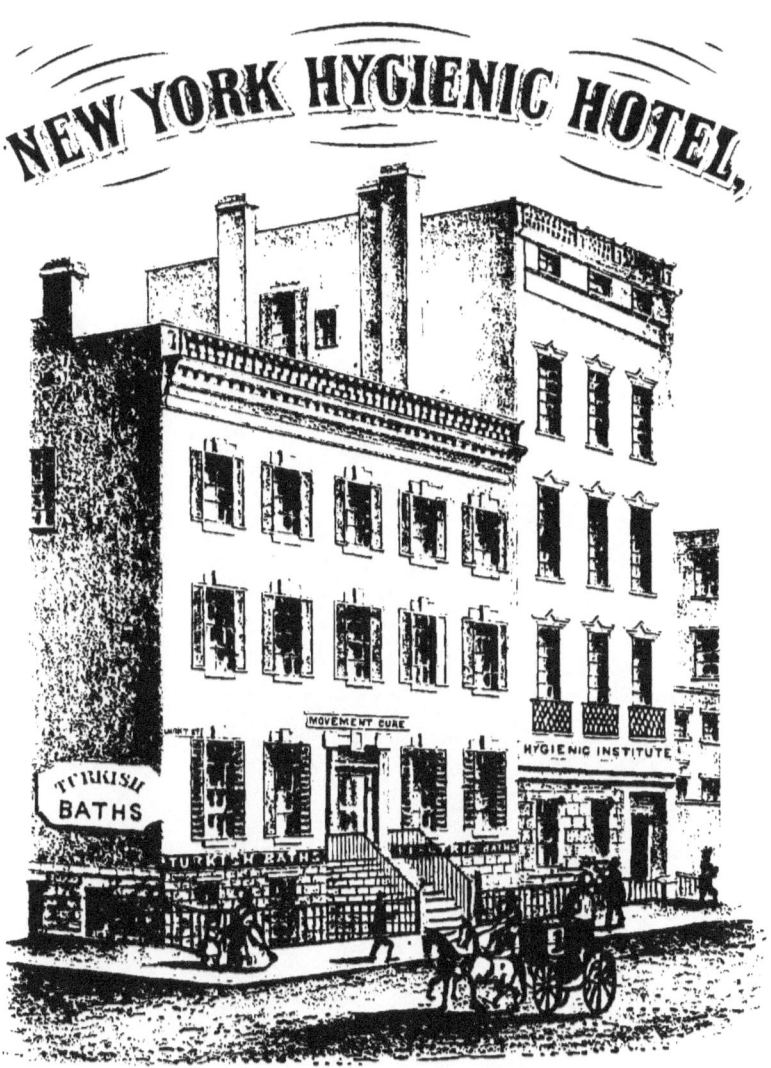

tion was founded in 1771 by the Earl of Dunmore, who was at that time Governor of the Colony. The Institution has an annual revenue of about eighty thousand dollars, from which the Hospital is sustained, together with those patients who are able to pay. A charge of four dollars per week secures the best of nursing and medicine. Visitors admitted from 10 A. M. till 5 P. M.

ST. LUKE'S HOSPITAL

Is situated at the corner of Fifth avenue and Fifty-eighth street. This Institution is under the management of members of the Episcopal Church. No creed, color, or nation, is rejected. Open to visitors daily.

JEWS' HOSPITAL,

As its name indicates, is sustained by the Jewish denomination. Located at 158 West Twenty-eighth street. Open to visitors from ten A. M. till six P. M.

BELLEVUE HOSPITAL

Is located at the foot of East Twenty-sixth street.

LIBRARIES.

It is always a source of gratification to find men, whose daily avocations are of the most bustling and industrial nature, availing themselves of every leisure interval to cultivate and increase their means of intellectual enjoyment and there can be no greater ornaments to a city than those literary and educational institutions which, springing from, and supported by, the people, are adapted to the public wants. It matters not whether the buildings are of brick, costly marble, or "plain rooms," their object consecrates and invests them with a host of pleasing associations. We especially allude to the many libraries located in various parts of our city, which are worthy to be compared with those of foreign countries as to the rare and valuable collections which they contain. Nearly all of these Libraries are accessible to strangers. A visit to these noble institutions, with their rich collection of books, will become a necessity to all who have any love for literature and art.

Astor Library.

This magnificent structure is located on Lafayette, near Astor place. Was founded by the munificence of John Jacob Astor, who left four hundred thousand dollars for that purpose. It contains about one hundred and twenty thousand volumes, of great variety and value. It is the largest library in the United States. Open to visitors from ten A. M. to 5 P. M.

Mercantile Library

Is situated in Astor place, Eighth street. This noble establishment has a fine library of sixty

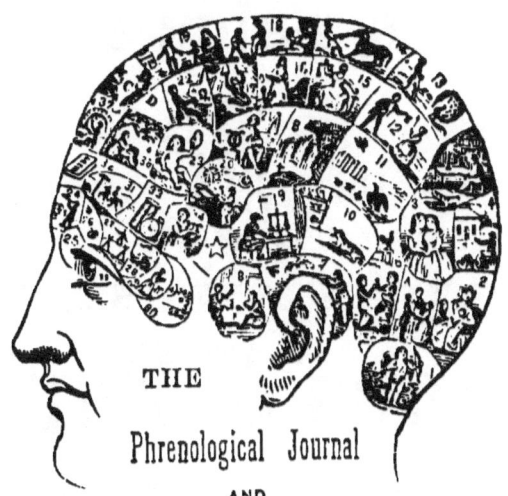

THE Phrenological Journal
AND
LIFE ILLUSTRATED.
A FIRST-CLASS MONTHLY.

Devoted to Physiognomy, Phrenology, Ethnology, Physiology, Psychology, Sociology, Education, Art, Literature; with measures to Reform, Elevate and Improve Mankind Physically and Spiritually. S. R. WELLS, Editor.

THE ILLUSTRATED PHRENOLOGICAL JOURNAL contains **Ethnology.**—The Natural History of Man. **Physiology.**—Heart, Lungs, Stomach, Nerves. **Phrenology.**—Temperaments and Brain. **Physiognomy.**—"Signs of Character and How to Read Them." **Psychology.**—"Science of the Soul." Man's Relations to this life, and the life to come. Monthly, $3 a year. Sample numbers 30 cts. New vols. begin July and January. Please address

S. R. WELLS, 389 Broadway, N. Y.

EDITORIAL AND OTHER NOTICES.

This Magazine, now ably edited by Mr. S. R. Wells, has steadily grown in public favor, and its counsels on subjects pertaining to health, education, and physical culture are sound, timely and emphatic.—*N. Y. Evening Post.*

Few works will better repay perusal in the family than this rich storehouse of instruction and entertainment, which never fails to illustrate the practical philosophy of life, with its lively expositions, appropriate anecdotes, and agreeable sketches of distinguished individuals.—*N. Y. Tribune.*

ADAMS, PRICE & CO'S.

TRADE MARK

"GUARANTEED"
Spoons & Forks,

Sales Room, 20 John Street,

New York.

The above firm are undoubtedly manufacturing at the present time the most DURABLE, as well as in other respects the most desirable Spoons and Forks in the market. They have succeeded in producing in Electro Plate all that softness and delicacy of finish, heretofore supposed to be peculiar to solid silver alone, and the most careful scrutiny cannot detect that their goods are not solid work. They are plated with pure silver on the finest quality of nickel silver, and the weight of plate is subjected to such careful tests that the firm make a standing offer of $1,000 for proof that any article of their manufacture and bearing their trade-mark is of a lower grade than that indicated by the stamp upon the back.

This firm also manufacture Dinner and Tea Services of the most reliable quality and beautiful design. Church Communion Ware, chaste, elegant and durable, is another specialty of the house.

A visit to their Works, No. 40 Columbia Street, Brooklyn, or their Sales Room, No. 20 John Street, New York, could not fail to be entertaining, instructive, and perhaps profitable to the visitor in the city

ACADEMY OF DESIGN.

thousand volumes, together with a reading-room, lecture-room and cabinet of minerals.

New York Society Library

Is located in University place, near Twelfth street. Contains a fine collection of books, numbering about forty-five thousand volumes.

City Library

Is in the City Hall. Accessible at all times.

New York Law Library

Contains a choice collection of books. Located at 41 Chamber street.

Apprentices' Library

Is located in Mechanics' Hall, 472 Broadway. Is for the use of Apprentices. Contains about twenty thousand volumes.

Mechanics' Library.

No. 20 Fourth avenue. Has over four thousand volumes.

Printers' Library.

No. 3 Chamber street. Contains five thousand volumes.

Women's Library

Is in the University building, opposite Washington square. Has a collection of nearly five thousand volumes.

BANKS.

There are in New York seventy Banks, with a capital of eighty-eight millions. Many of the Bank buildings are beautiful specimens of architecture, especially those of the Bank of the Republic, New York, Mechanics, America, Manhattan, City, Union, National, North America, on Wall street; Metropolitan, American Exchange, Shoe and Leather, and Pacific, on Broadway; Nassau, and Bank of Commerce, on Nassau street.

TELEGRAPH OFFICES

Are located at 145 Broadway, with branch offices at all the leading hotels and railroad depots.

ODD FELLOWS' HALL.

The most imposing Hall of the "Order" is located on the corner of Centre and Grand streets. It is constructed of brown stone, in the Egyptian, Grecian and Elizabethan style of architecture. Erected in 1849, and cost one hundred and twenty-five thousand dollars. It is well worthy a visit. Strangers admitted second Tuesday in each month.

MONUMENTS.

New York does not contain any monuments of very special note as works of art. The following, however, are worthy to be visited:

HENRY WELSH,
WHOLESALE GROCER,
TEA DEALER,
AND
Commission Merchant,

321 Washington St.   23 & 25 Jay St.
and 334 Greenwich St.

Taylor's Building,

New York.

FREEMAN & BURR,
CLOTHIERS,
Merchant Tailors
AND
OUTFITTERS,
IN
GENTLEMEN'S AND BOYS' CLOTHING
OF EVERY DESCRIPTION.
FURNISHING GOODS, ETC.

The Best Foreign and Domestic Fabrics
ALWAYS IN STOCK FOR ORDERS AND TO MEASURE.

FREEMAN & BURR,

No. 124 FULTON ST. & 90 NASSAU ST.

(*S. E. Corner Fulton and Nassau Streets,*)

New York.

DENNISON & CO.

198 Broadway, New York,

MANUFACTURERS OF

Merchandise Tags,

DIRECTION LABELS, AND SHIPPING CARDS,

Dry Goods Tickets and Gum Labels,

FANCY TICKETS, ETC.

AGENTS FOR SALE OF

FAY'S PATENT HOOK TAGS,

JEWELERS' FINDINGS,

CONSISTING OF

PAPER BOXES

of all kinds adapted to the trade,

JEWELERS' CARDS,

Plain (and cut for Buttons, etc.)

PINK AND WHITE COTTON,

Fine Twines, Tissue Papers. Chamois Skins, Plain and Rouged.

---

198 Broadway, New York.

36 South Third St., Phila.   &   66 Milk Street, Boston.

FIFTH AVENUE HOTEL.

Sugar-House Martyrs' Monument.

In Trinity church-yard stands the monumental tribute of the Church corporation to the honored "Sugar-House Martyrs." It is constructed of finely-cut and ornamented brown stone, presenting a graceful appearance, while it attracts the especial interest of every American patriot, from the fact that the ground immediately under and around it is rich with the ashes of our Revolutionary fathers.

Washington Equestrian Statue.

This bronze statue of the Father of his Country, by H. K. Brown, erected at a cost of thirty thousand dollars, is situated in Union square, enclosed by an iron railing.

Worth Monument,

Constructed of granite, forty feet high, in memory of General Worth, who fell in the war with Mexico, is located in Madison square, opposite Fifth Avenue Hotel.

FORTS AND FORTIFICATIONS.

There are quite a number of these objects of interest in the vicinity of New York, located as follows:

Fort Lafayette,

Rendered famous from its being the receptacle for State prisoners during the recent war, is situated about eight miles down the bay, in the Narrows.

Fort Hamilton,

Located opposite, on the Long Island shore, is a very fine fort, with two tier of casemates.

Fort Richmond,

On the Staten Island shore, opposite to Fort Lafayette, is the largest and handsomest structure of the kind around New York. It has four tier of casemates, and is pierced for about one hundred and eighty guns.

Fort Columbus

Is situated on the centre of Governor's Island.

Castle William

Is also located on Governor's Island at the water's edge—a round tower, six hundred feet in circumference, sixty feet high, with three tier of guns.

Fort Wood

Is located on Bedloe's Island, in the bay, opposite to Governor's Island.

Fort Schuyler

Is situated on Long Island Sound, fourteen miles from New York.

Fort Tompkins,

On Staten Island, in the rear of Fort Richmond, on an elevation of two hundred and fifty feet.

B. F. BEEKMAN & CO.

IMPORTERS AND MANUFACTURERS OF

STRAW AND SILK GOODS,

Flowers, Feathers, &c.

No. 377 Broadway, Corner White St.

(Up-Stairs.)

New York.

A. H. ROSENHEIM,

WHOLESALE DEALER IN

RIBBONS

AND

MILLINERY PIECE GOODS,

No. 391 BROADWAY,

New York.

BARDWELL & HOPKINS,

COMMISSION MERCHANTS,

28 WARREN STREET,

NEW YORK.

Agents for Arms & Bardwell Manufacturing Company's
PATENT SELF-CLOSING POCKET-BOOKS, MEMO-
RANDUMS AND DIARIES.

The "PAISLEY" SOFT-FINISHED MACHINE-THREAD, &c.
The "ANCHOR" STAY BINDING and TAPES.

ESTABLISHED IN 1835.

J. HOWARD FOOTE,

Successor to

ROHÉ & LEAVITT,

IMPORTER AND WHOLESALE DEALER IN

MUSICAL INSTRUMENTS,

STRINGS,

Brass and German Silver Band Instruments,

AND

MUSICAL MERCHANDISE OF EVERY DESCRIPTION.

Musical Boxes

CONSTANTLY ON HAND.

A superb assortment of these charming instruments, *made expressly for this house by the best Swiss and French makers.*

PRINCIPAL HOUSE,
    31 Maiden Lane, New York.

BRANCH HOUSE,
    Nos. 47 & 49 Dearborn Street, Chicago.

PLACES OF AMUSEMENT.

Wallack's Theatre, located corner of Broadway and Thirteenth street.
Niblo's Garden, in the rear of Metropolitan Hotel. Entrance, Broadway.
Winter Garden is on Broadway, opposite Bond street.
Olympic Theatre, 622 Broadway.
Theatre Comique is located at 514 Broadway.
French Theatre, Fourteenth street, near Fifth avenue.
Old Bowery Theatre, 46 Bowery, near Canal street.
Stadt Theatre, located in the Bowery, opposite Old Bowery Theatre.
Broadway Theatre, 483 Broadway, corner Broome street.
Butler's Theatre, 472 Broadway.
San Francisco Minstrels, 585 Broadway.
Bunyan Hall, Fifteenth street and Broadway.
New York Circus, Fourteenth street, opposite Academy of Music.
Kelly & Leon's Minstrels, 720 Broadway.
Fifth Avenue Opera House, 4 West Twenty-fourth street.
Tony Pastor's Opera House, 201 Bowery.
Barnum's Museum, Broadway, above Spring street.

New York Theatre, 730 Broadway.
Terrace Gardens, corner Third avenue and Fifty-ninth street.
Steinway's Hall, 73 East Fourteenth street.
Irving Hall, Irving Place, opposite Academy of Music.
Academy of Music, corner of East Fourteenth and Irving Place.
Pike's Opera House, Eighth Avenue and Twenty-third street.
Banvard's Theatre, Broadway and Thirtieth street.
Museum of Anatomy, 618 Broadway.
Studio Building, Tenth street, near Sixth avenue.
Art Gallery, Cooper's Institute, Eighth street and Third avenue.

CHAS. H. DITSON & CO.
(*Successors* to *FIRTH, SON & Co.*)
MUSIC PUBLISHERS,
AND DEALERS IN
SHEET MUSIC, MUSIC BOOKS,
AND MUSICAL MERCHANDISE,
No. 711 BROADWAY,

OLIVER DITSON.
JOHN C. HAYNES.
CHAS. H. DITSON.
}   New York.

PIANOS, ORGANS, AND MELODEONS TO LET.

MOSELEY'S CORRUGATED IRON BUILDING.

Models of Bridge and other work, to be seen at our Office.

116 WILLIAM STREET, NEW YORK.

See page 93.

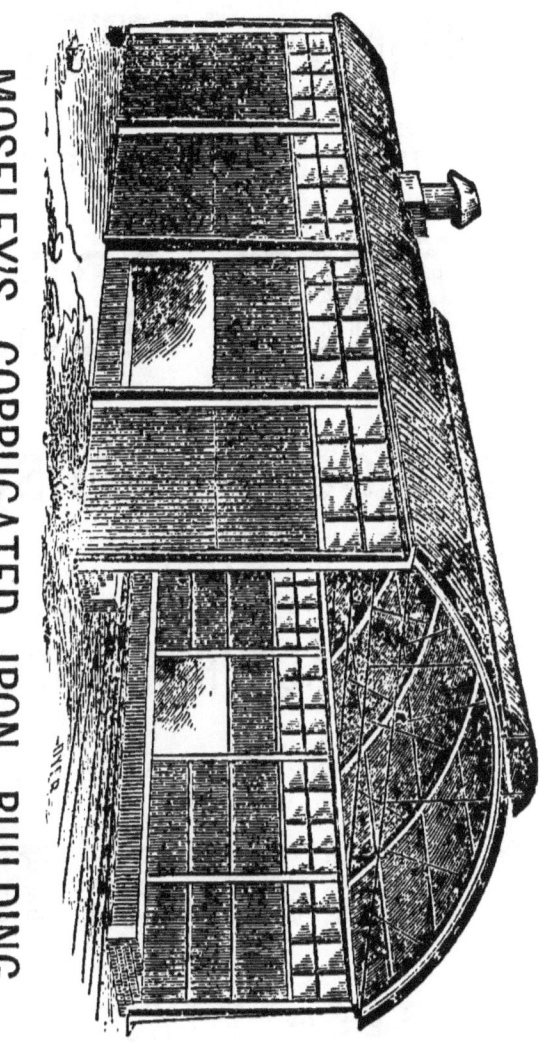

HASTINGS, POTTER & CO.

IMPORTERS AND DEALERS IN

FANCY GOODS,

Yankee Notions, &c.

ALSO,

MANUFACTURERS' AGENTS

AND DEALERS IN

JEWELRY,

Sleeve-Buttons, &c.

100 Chamber Street,

New York.

ALMS HOUSE BUILDINGS,
Blackwells Island.

NEWSPAPERS.

The achievements of the last fifty years have been such that no local or temporary interest can satisfy the mind; everything is conducted on a grand scale. The extension of education, the progress of science, the facilities of communication and intercourse between nations, and, above all, the freedom of the Press, and its consequent wide and rapid circulation of news, has served to produce this extent of thought and purpose. In the United States the Press is supremely important. The activity and power of the Newspaper Press of the United States date their origin from the Revolutionary war. Previous to that event they were few in number, and barren of that interest, vigor and originality, so important a feature in those of the present day. Great Britain and the United Colonies having determined to settle their dispute by arms, both appealed to the people. Each had their partisans; but there were many independent or indifferent persons, whose support was valuable. Then it was the Press entered into the strife, and assumed that direction of public opinion which has continued ever since, and formed so remarkable a feature in modern political history.

There are about sixteen daily papers published in this city, the principal ones of which are—

JOURNAL OF COMMERCE,	TRANSCRIPT,
HERALD,	POST (Evening),
TIMES,	EXPRESS (Evening),
TRIBUNE,	ABEND ZEITUNG (German),
WORLD,	DEMOCRAT (German),
COMMERCIAL ADVERTISER,	STADTS ZEITUNG (German),
NEWS,	COURRIER DES ETATS UNIS
SUN,	(French).

There are also one hundred and twenty weekly papers.

CHURCHES.

There are in the City of New York three hundred and fifty churches, very many of which are noted for their elegance and architectural beauty.

Baptist.

Antioch.   264 Bleecker street.
First.   354 Broome street.
Fifth Avenue.   Near W. Forty-sixth street.
Calvary.   50 West Twenty-third street.
Lexington Avenue.   Near East Thirty-seventh street.
Sixth Street.   211 Sixth street.
Berean.   35 Downing street.
Cannon Street.   317 Madison street.
Bethlehem   395 West Forty-fifth street.
Ebenezer.   154 West Thirty-sixth street.

EVERETT HOUSE.

A. HILL & CO.

Wholesale Commission Dealers in

CARPETS,

Floor, Table, and Stair

OIL CLOTHS,

Mats, Mattings,

BINDINGS, THREAD, &c.

261 CANAL STREET,

(Between Broadway and Earle's Hotel,)

NEW YORK.

First Mariners'. Oliver, corner Henry street.
South. 147 West Twenty-fifth street.
Tabernacle. 162 Second avenue.
Fifth Avenue. Near One Hundred and Twenty-Sixth street.
Sixteenth Street. 257 West Sixteenth street.
North. 126 Christopher street.
Yorkville. Eighty-third st., near Second avenue.
Laight Street. Corner Varick street.
Bethesda. Fifty-third, near Seventh avenue.
Freewill. 74 West Seventeenth street.
Zion. (Colored.) 155 Sullivan street.
Abyssinian. (Colored.) 166 Waverly place.
Bloomingdale. 220 West Forty-second street.
Madison Avenue. Corner E. Thirty-first street.
Amity Street. 161 Fifth avenue.
McDougal Street. 24 McDougal street.
Stanton. 36 Stanton street.
Welsh. 141 Chrystie street.
Pilgrim. Thirty-third st., near Eighth avenue.

Congregational.

Church of the Puritans. Union place corner Fifteenth street.
Welsh. 33 E. Eleventh street.
Bethesda. (Colored.) 681 Sixth avenue, corner Thirty-fourth street.
Tabernacle. Sixth avenue, corner Thirty-fourth street.
St. John's. Forty-first st., near Sixth avenue.

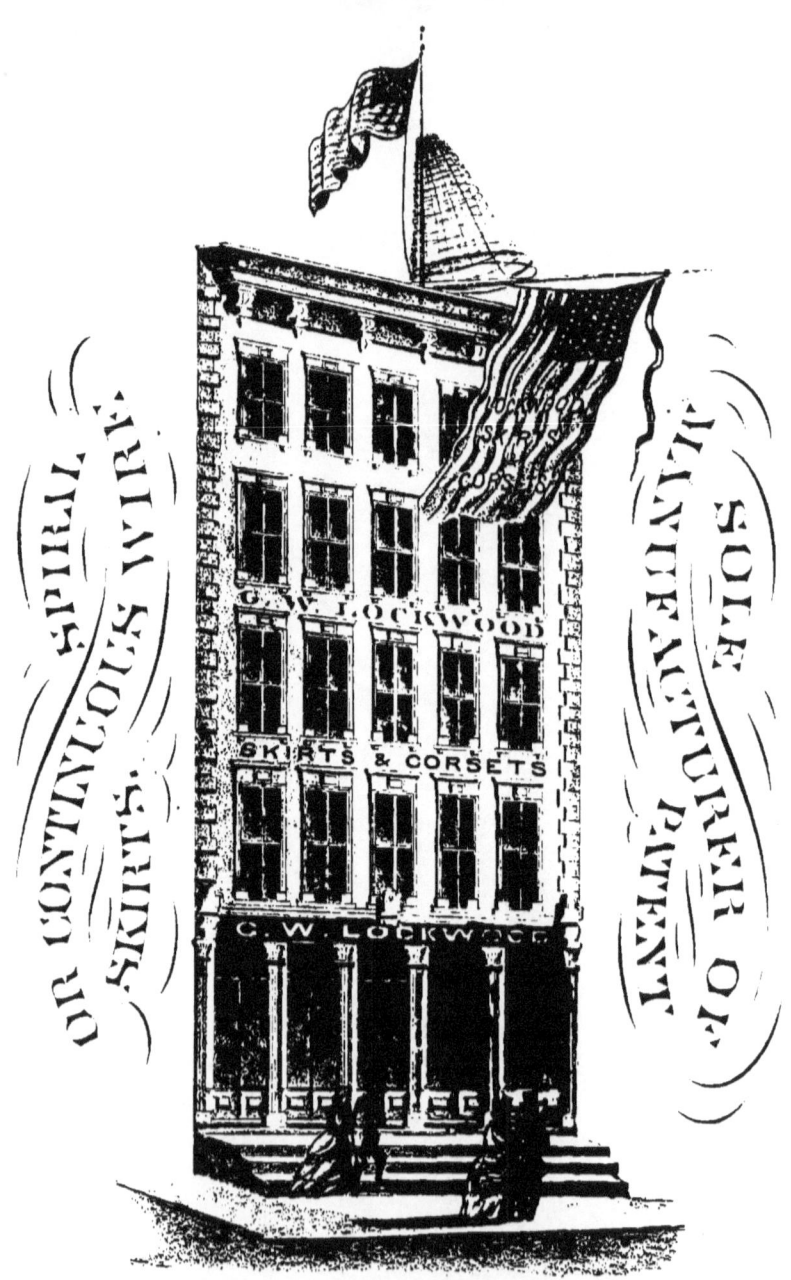

Dutch Reformed.

Collegiate.   Forty-eighth st., near Fifth avenue.
Collegiate.   Fifth avenue, corner Twenty-ninth street.
Collegiate.   Lafayette place.
Market Street.   Corner Henry.
German Reformed.   129 Norfolk street.
Northwest.   145 West Twenty-third street.
German Evangelical.   141 East Houston street.
Union.   25 Sixth avenue street.
Washington Square.   Wooster street.
Harlem.   Third avenue, corner One Hundred and Twenty-first street.
Fourth German.   112 West Twenty-ninth street.
Prospect Hill.   Third avenue, near Eighty-seventh street.
South.   Fifth avenue, corner Twenty-first street.
Mount Pleasant.   158 East Fiftieth street.
Thirty-fourth Street.   Near Eighth avenue.
Greenwich.   53 West Forty-sixth street.
Twenty-first Street.   47 West Twenty-first street.
Bloomingdale.   Broadway, corner Sixty-eighth street.
Collegiate.   Fulton, corner William street.
Manhattan.   71 Avenue B.

Lutheran.

St. Luke's.   208 West Forty-third street.
Avenue B.   Corner Ninth street.
St. John's.   81 Christopher street.
St. Paul's.   226 Sixth avenue.

St. Peter's. 125 East Fiftieth street.
St. Marcus. 52 Sixth avenue.
Yorkville. Eighty-seventh st., near Fourth av'e.
St. Matthew's. Walker street.
St. James. 103 East Fifteenth street.

Methodist Episcopal.

Thirty-seventh Street. 129 E. Thirty-seventh street.
Seventh Street. 24 Seventh street.
Bedford Street. 28 Morton street.
Tenth Avenue. 426 Tenth avenue.
Alanson. 52 Norfolk street.
Jane Street. 13 Jane street.
Hedding. 170 East Seventeenth street.
Second Street. 276 Second street.
Beekman Hill. Fiftieth st., near Second avenue.
Thirtieth Street. 207 West Thirtieth street.
St. Paul's. Fourth avenue, corner Twenty-second street.
Eighteenth Street. 193 West Eighteenth street.
Central. 44 Seventh avenue.
Yorkville. Eighty-Sixth st., near Fourth avenue.
Swedish Bethel. Pier Eleven, North river.
Trinity. 248 West Thirty-fourth street.
Forsyth Street. 10 Forsyth street.
Forty-third Street. 177 West Forty-third street.
Willett Street. 7 Willett street.
St. John's. 133 West Fifty-third street.
Mission. 61 Park street.
Harlem. One Hundred and Twenty-fifth street, near Third avenue.

Lexington Avenue.   Corner Fifty-second street.
Second Avenue.   Corner One Hundred and Nineteenth street.
Duane.   294 Hudson street.
John Street.   44 John street.
Washington Square.   Fourth street.
Allen Street.   126 Allen street.
Twenty-fourth Street.   Near Ninth avenue.
Rose Hill.   125 East Twenty-seventh street.
Greene Street.   59 Greene street.
Jane's Mission.   461 West Forty-fourth street.
West Harlem.   One Hundred and Twenty-fifth street, near Sixth avenue.

African Methodist Episcopal.

Bethel.   214 Sullivan street.
Zion.   331 Bleecker street.
Union.   161 West Fifteenth street.

Methodist Protestant.

First.   87 Attorney street.

Presbyterian.

Madison Square.   Corner East Twenty-fourth street.
Fifteenth Street.   Near Third avenue.
French.   9 University place.
Fiftieth Street.   Near Eighth avenue.
Mercer Street.   Near Eighth street.
Yorkville.   147 East Eighty-sixth street.
Thirteenth Street.   Near Seventh avenue.

Twenty-third Street. Near Seventh avenue.
Fourth Avenue. Corner Twenty-second street.
Central. Broome, near Elm street.
Prince Street. (Colored.) Corner Marion st.
University Place. Corner Tenth street.
West. Forty-second street, near Fifth avenue.
Eleventh. Fifty-fifth st., near Lexington avenue.
African Union. (Colored.) 157 West Twenty-eighth street.
Westminster. 151 West Twenty-second street.
Rutgers street. Madison avenue, cor. Twenty-ninth street.
Scotch. 53 West Fourteenth street.
Eighty-fourth Street. Near Bloomingdale road.
Mission. 419 Third avenue.
Covenant. Park avenue, corner Thirty-fifth street.
Allen Street. 61 Allen street.
Fifth Avenue. Corner Nineteenth street.
Mission. 107 Seventh avenue.
Lexington Avenue. Corner East Forty-sixth street.
Forty-second Street. 233 West Forty-second street.
Manhattanville. One Hundred and Twenty-sixth street, corner Ninth avenue.
Mission. Thirty-third st., corner Eighth avenue.
Chelsea. 353 West Twenty-second street.
Seventh. Broome, corner Ridge.
Brick. Fifth avenue, corner Thirty-seventh st.
German. 290 Madison street.

EARLE'S HOUSE.

N. W. BURTIS & CO.

IMPORTERS AND JOBBERS OF

FANCY GOODS, NOTIONS, HOSIERY, GLOVES, FANCY KNIT WOOLLENS, PERFUMERY,

WATCHES, JEWELRY, &c.

NOS. 250 & 252 CANAL STREET

(Opposite Earl's Hotel,)

NEW YORK.

With abundant facilities for doing a business to the interest of purchasers, and a guarantee of quick and close attention to PACKING and SHIPPING goods, and the careful FILLING of ORDERS, we ask that our friends and buyers generally, will call and judge themselves of the advantages we can offer them from a STOCK unsurpassed in *variety, quality* and *price.*

North.   Ninth avenue, corner Thirty-first street.
Twenty-eighth Street.   252 W. Twenty-eighth st
Grand Street.   Thirty-fourth st. near Broadway.
Spring Street.   246 Spring street.
Covenant. (Colored.)   231 W. Sixteenth street.
Canal Street.   7 Greene street.
First.   Fifth avenue, corner Eleventh street.
Fourteenth Street.   Corner Second avenue.

United Presbyterian.

Third.   41 Charles street.
Jane Street.   41 Jane street.
Seventh.   434 West Forty-fourth street.
Seventh Avenue.   29 Seventh avenue.
Eleventh Street.   33 East Eleventh street.
Twenty-fifth Street.   161 West Twenty-fifth st.

Associate Reformed Presbyterian.

Fourth.   157 Thompson street.

Reformed Presbyterian.

Second.   Clinton Hall.
First.   123 West Twelfth street.
Sullivan Street.   101 Sullivan street.
Third.   238 West Twenty-third street.
Second.   167 West Eleventh street.

Protestant Episcopal.

St. Mary's.   Manhattanville.
Anthon Memorial.   103 West Forty-eighth st.
St. Luke's.   483 Hudson street.
St. Peter's.   224 West Twentieth street.

BUY, SELL AND EXCHANGE.

All issues of U.S. BONDS on the most liberal terms. *GOLD* bought & sold at *MARKET RATES, COUPONS CASHED.* **STOCKS** BOUGHT & SOLD ON COMMISSION FOR **CASH**. *ACCOUNTS* received & *INTEREST* allowed on Balances subject to *CHECK* at sight.

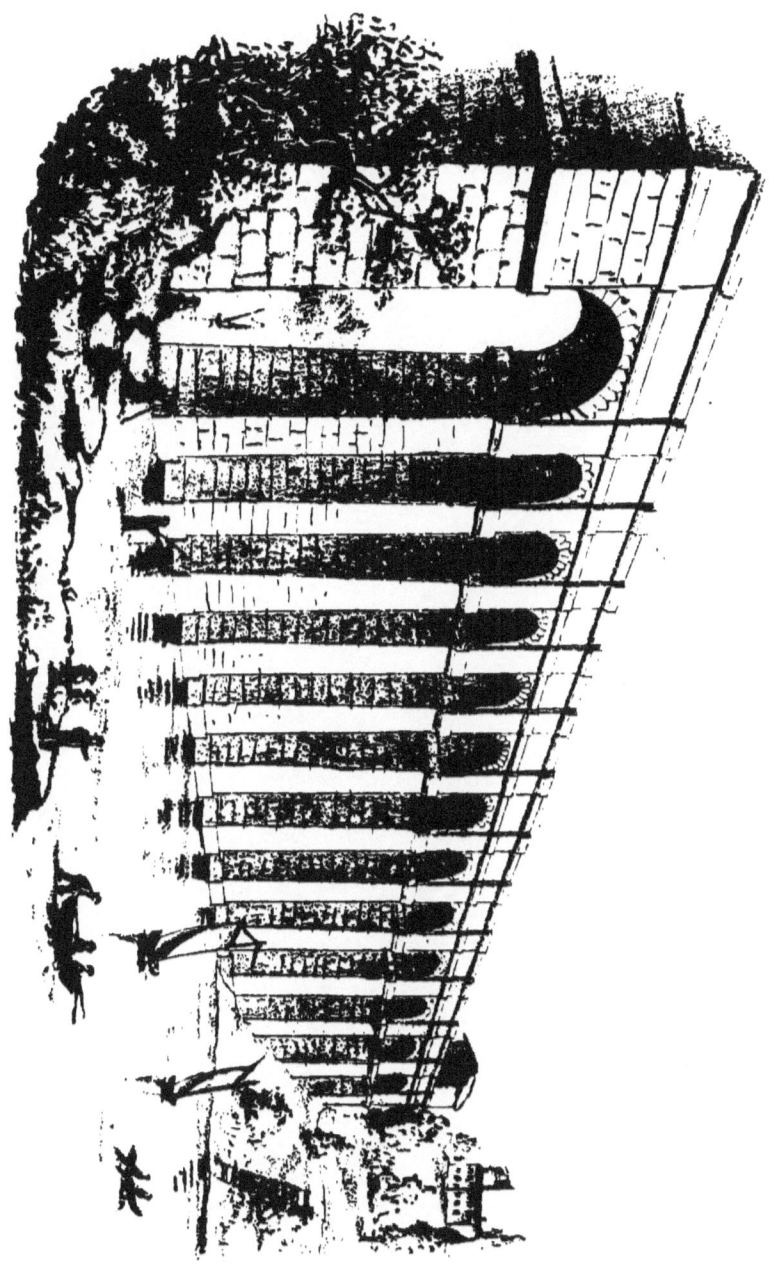

HIGH BRIDGE.

St. Ann's.   7 West Eighteenth street.
Zion Chapel.   557 Third avenue.
St. James'.   East Sixty-ninth, near Third ave.
Church of the Nativity.   70 Avenue C.
Mission.   176 West Eighteenth street.
St. Bartholomew's.   Lafayette place.
All Saints.   286 Henry street.
Church of the Annunciation.   110 West Fourteenth street.
St. Matthias.   Broadway, corner Thirty-second street.
Redemption.   98 East Fourteenth street.
Trinity.   Broadway, opposite Wall street.
St. John Baptist.   231 Lexington avenue.
St. Clement's.   108 Amity street.
Holy Innocents'.   94 West Thirty-seventh st.
Christ.   Fifth avenue, corner Thirty-fifth street.
Resurrection.   65 West Thirty-fifth street.
St. Mark's Mission.   141 Avenue A.
St. Luke's.   483 Hudson street.
St. Ann's.   7 West Eighteenth.
St. Timothy's.   Fifty-fourth, near Eighth ave.
St. Paul's.   Broadway, corner Vesey street.
Advent.   725 Sixth avenue.
Trinity Chapel.   15 West Twenty-fifth street.
Transfiguration.   Twenty-ninth st., near Fifth avenue.
Holy Apostles.   Ninth avenue, corner Twenty-eighth street.
Good Shepherd.   Fifty-fourth Street, near Second avenue.

7 *

Reconciliation. 150 East Thirty-first street.
Mediator. Lexington avenue, corner Thirtieth street.
Holy Communion. Sixth avenue, corner Twentieth street.
St. George the Martyr. 39 West Forty-fourth street.
Our Saviour. Foot of Pike street.
Church of the Holy Martyrs. 39 Forsyth st.
Church of the Incarnation. Madison avenue, corner Thirty-fifth street.
St. Philip's. (Colored.) 305 Mulberry street.
St. Alban's. Lexington avenue.
Church of Holy Communion. Sixth avenue, corner Twentieth street.
Twenty-ninth Street. Near Ninth avenue.
St. Michael's. Broadway, corner Ninty-ninth street.
All Angels. Eighty-first st., near Eleventh ave.
St. Stephen's. 120 Christie street.
St. George's Chapel. Beekman, corner Cliff st.
Holy Comforter. Foot of Hubert street.
St. George's. (German.) Fourteenth street near First avenue.
Annunciation. 110 West Fourteenth street.
St. Paul's. Harlem.
Mission. 117 Thompson street.
Ascension. Fifth avenue, corner Tenth street
Intercession. One Hundred and Fifty-fourth street, corner Tenth avenue.
Yorkville. Yorkville.

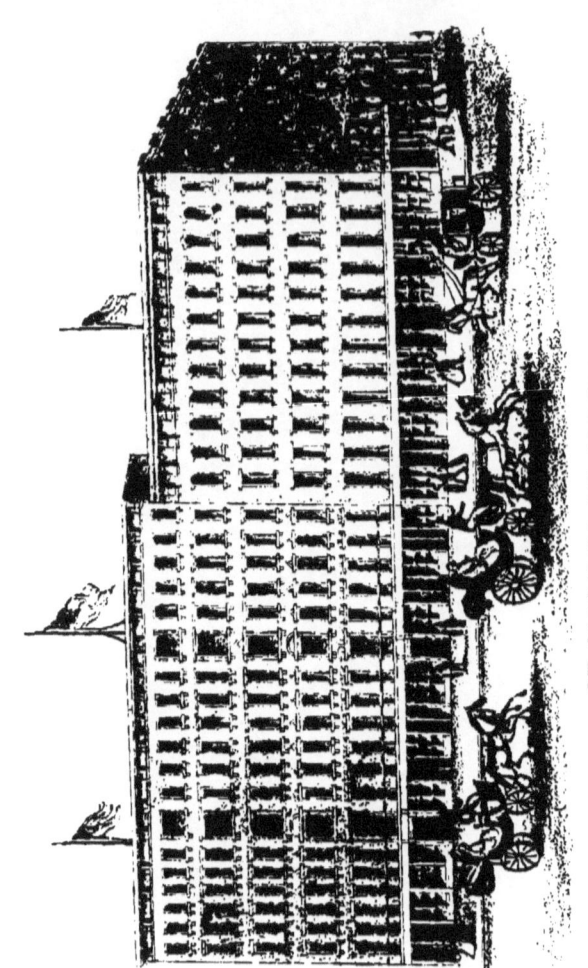

CHAS. H. GRIFFIN & CO.

360 BROADWAY AND 67 FRANKLIN STREET,

New York.

CLOTHS, CASSIMERES, CLOAKINGS, TRIMMINGS,

BLACK SILKS, ETC.

Zion. Madison avenue, corner Thirty-eighth st.
Mission. 220 East Nineteenth street.
Mission. 256 Madison street.
Grace. 800 Broadway.
Redeemer. Eighty-fifth st., near Second avenue.
St. Luke's. 483 Hudson street.
St. George's. Rutherford place.
Holy Trinity. Madison avenue, corner Forty-second street.
Du St. Esprit. 30 West Twenty-second street.
St. Mark's. Stuyvesant street.
Mission. 133 East Twenty-third street.
Calvary. Fourth avenue, corner Twenty-first st.
St. John's. 46 Varick street.
Messiah. (Colored.) 102 Mercer street.
St. John Evangelist. 20 Hammond street.
Union. (Colored.) Second avenue, near Eighty-fourth street.
Mission. Eighty-fourth st., near Fourth avenue.

Roman Catholic.

St. Teresa. Rutgers street, corner Henry.
Annunciation. One Hundred and Thirty-first street, near Broadway.
St. James'. 32 James street.
St. Paul's. One Hundred and Seventeenth street, near Fourth avenue.
St. Gabriel's. Thirty-seventh street, near Second avenue.
St. Stephen's. 93 East Twenty-eighth street.
St. Andrew's. Duane st., corner City Hall place.

PACIFIC MUTUAL INSURANCE COMPANY

No. 111 BROADWAY.

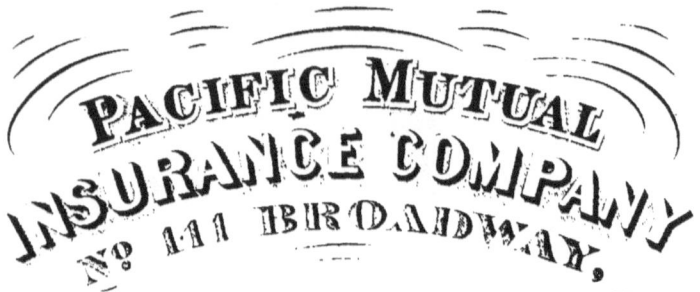

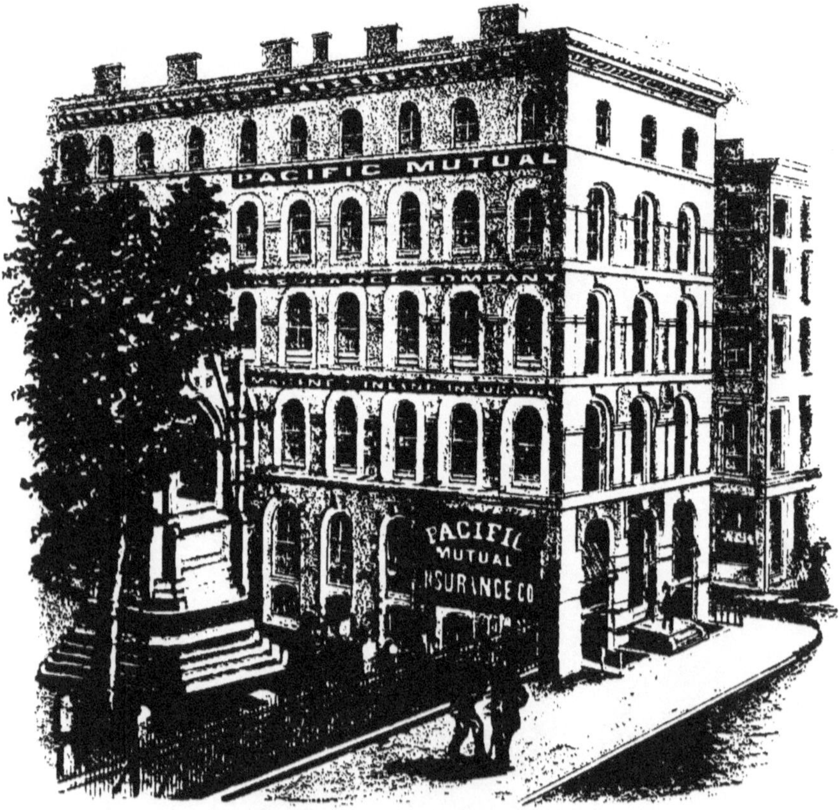

TRINITY BUILDING

NEW YORK.

ASSETS OVER $1.000.000.

AVERAGE PROFITS IN 13 YEARS OVER 27 PER CENT.

St. John Baptist. (German.) 125 West Thirtieth street.
St. Michael's. 265 West Thirty-first street.
St. Joseph's. Sixth avenue, corner West Washington place.
St. Joseph's. (German.) One Hundred and Twenty-fifth street, corner Ninth avenue.
St. Paul's. Fifty-ninth st., corner Ninth avenue.
St. Nicholas. (German.) 125 Second street.
St. Vincent de Paul. 127 West Twenty-third st.
St. Francis Xavier. 36 W. Sixteenth street.
St. Columbia. 339 W. Twenty-fifth street.
Holy Cross. 335 W. Forty-second street.
Nativity. 46 Second avenue.
St. Patrick's. Mott street.
St. Mary's. 438 Grand street.
St. John Evangelist. Fiftieth street, near Fifth avenue.
St. Bridget's. Avenue B, corner Eighth street.
Immaculate Conception. 245 E. Fourteenth st.
St. Lawrence. Eighty-fourth street, near Fourth avenue.
St. Boniface. Forty-seventh street, near Second avenue.
Most Holy Redeemer. 165 Third street.
St. Francis. (German.) 93 West Thirty-first st.
St. Ann's. 149 Eighth street.
Assumption. Forty-ninth street, near Ninth avenue.
St. Peter's. Barclay, corner Church street.
Transfiguration. Mott, corner Park street.

Unitarian.

All-Soul's. Fourth avenue, corner Twentieth street.
Third. Fortieth street, near Sixth avenue.
Messiah. Madison avenue, corner Twenty-eighth street.

Universalist.

Sixth. 116 West Twentieth street.
Fourth. Fifth avenue, corner Forty-fifth street.
Second. Second avenue, corner Eleventh street.
Third. 206 Bleecker street.

Miscellaneous.

Christian Israelites. 108 First street.
German Evangelical Reformed. 97 Suffolk street.
Wesleyan Methodist. 235 West Forty-eighth st.
Disciples'. 24 West Twenty-eighth street.
Congregational Methodist. West Twenty-fourth street, near Sixth avenue.
Evangelical. 108 West Twenty-fourth street.
Catholic Apostolic. 128 West Sixteenth street.
Swedenborgian. 68 East Thirty-fifth street.
Messiah. 7 Seventh avenue.
Moravian. Fourth avenue, corner Twenty-third street.
Mariners'. Madison street, corner Catharine street.
Welsh. 133 East Thirteenth street.
Second Advent. 68 East Broadway.
Friends' Meeting-houses. 15th st., bet. 2d and 3d av.; 27th st., bet. 6th av. and Broadway; 20th st., bet. 3d and 4th av. (Orthodox.)

Religious and Miscellaneous Institutions.

Young Men's Christian Association, 161 Fifth avenue.
American Tract Society, 150 Nassau street.
American Baptist Free Mission Society, 37 Park Row.
American Bible Society, No. 4 Bible House.
American Bible Union, 350 Broome street.
American Board of Com. for Foreign Missions, 4 Bible House.
American Female Guardian Society, 29 East Twenty-ninth street.
American Home Missionary Society, 11 Bible House.
American Seamen's Friends' Society, 80 Wall street.
American Sunday-school Union, 599 Broadway.
American and Foreign Bible Society, 116 Nassau street.
American Christian Union, 156 Chamber street.
Board of Mission of Reformed Dutch Church, 103 Fulton street.
Methodist Book Concern, 200 Mulberry street.
National Freedman's Association, 76 John street.
National Temperance Society, 172 William street.
New York Bible Society, 7 Beekman street.
New York Christian Alliance, 15 Reade street.
New York City Mission, 30 Bible House.
Presbyterian Board of Missions, 23 Centre street.
Prison Association, 12 Centre street.

BAUMS & KAHN,

Importers of
FRENCH
AND
GERMAN
FANCY BASKETS.

Manufacturers of
CANE AND WILLOW FURNITURE,
24 COURTLANDT STREET,

New York.

CONANT BROS.
MANUFACTURERS OF
LOOKING-GLASSES,
Portable Writing–Desks, and Fancy Boxes,
No. 12 COURTLANDT STREET,
(near Broadway,)

New York.

Factory at Mount Vernon, N. H.

WILDER'S PATENT
SALAMANDER SAFES,
Express and Specie Boxes,
WILDER SALAMANDER SAFE CO.
Depot, 15 COURTLANDT ST.,

New York.

SOUTHERN HOTEL.

Fine Clothing

FOR

MEN AND BOYS.

You will save *Twenty per Cent.* by purchasing at the

ONE PRICE

CASH

CLOTHING WAREHOUSES

OF

HYATT, HAGERMAN & CO.

611 Broadway, Cor. Houston St.

AND

122 Fulton Street,

New York.

Protestant Episcopal Tract Society, 5 Cooper Institute.

St. George's Society, 40 Exchange place.

Young Men's Howard Association, 196 Broadway.

Athenæum Club, 23 Union place.

New York Chess Club, University Building.

Century Club, 42 East Fifteenth street.

Sketch Club, University Building.

Lyceum of Natural History, Fourth avenue, near Fourteenth street.

Harmonic Society, 288 Fourth avenue.

New York State Colonization Society, 22 Bible House.

Artists' Fund Society, 52 East Twenty-third street.

American Institute, Cooper Institute.

HOTELS.

New York is justly noted for the number and elegance of its Hotels. There are about thirty of these magnificent establishments on Broadway. To the leading ones in the city will we direct attention.

Astor House.

This colossal edifice, located on Broadway, between Vesey and Barclay streets, was erected in 1836. It is built of solid granite, in the Doric order, with a front on Broadway of one hundred and eighty feet, and a depth of one hundred and twenty, of five stories high, at a cost of six hundred thousand dollars. It has accommodations for seven hundred guests. The Astor is the oldest of our first-class Hotels, and, since it was opened, has well sustained its high reputation

St. Nicholas.

This monument of architectural beauty is located corner of Broadway and Spring street. It is built of marble, in the Corinthian order, six stories high, two hundred feet front on Broadway, with a facade of surpassing elegance. It contains six hundred rooms, and can accommodate one thousand guests. The appointments in the St. Nicholas are without a fault; every thing being gotten up with a splendor and sumptuousness unequalled. Building erected in 1854, at a cost of one million dollars. As a security against fire, the whole establishment can be deluged with water in five minutes.

Metropolitan

Is situated on Broadway, corner of Prince street. This palatial structure, of brown stone, six stories high, was erected in 1850, at a cost of nine hundred thousand dollars. It is furnished throughout in the most splendid and expensive style, having all the accommodations and conveniences that the most luxurious taste could desire. Has about seven hundred rooms, and can accommodate one thousand guests.

HALL, ELTON & CO.
(ESTABLISHED 1837,)

MANUFACTURERS OF

Albata, German Silver & Plated Goods,

CONSISTING OF

Spoons, Forks, Soup-Ladles, Butter-Knives, Tea-Sets, Urns, Cake-Baskets, Castors, Butter-Coolers, Ice-Pitchers, &c.

Salesroom, 36 **PARK ROW, NEW YORK.**

Manufactory, WALLINGFORD, CONN.

SPECIE AND BANKING OFFICE
OF
GEO. D. ARTHUR & CO.
34 WALL STREET, NEW YORK,

Buy and Sell

Gold and Silver on the most favorable terms. Collections made in all parts of the United States and Canada.

Gold for Duties always ready for immediate delivery.

INTEREST ALLOWED ON DEPOSITS.

PRATT & SEYMOUR,

IMPORTERS AND JOBBERS OF

CARPETINGS,

Oil Cloths, Mattings, &c.

335 BROADWAY,

(Corner of Worth Street,)

New York.

WM. PRATT.   JAMES C. SEYMOUR.

Fifth Avenue.

This immense establishment, of white marble, located on Fifth avenue, opposite Madison square, occupies one of the finest sites in New York. It was erected by Mr. Paran Stevens, the well-known hotel proprietor, in 1858, at a cost of nine hundred thousand dollars. It is furnished throughout with an elegance and sumptuousness unequalled by any Hotel on this continent, and all its internal appointments and conveniences are unsurpassed. Has accommodations for eight hundred guests. All the rooms are well lighted and ventilated, and ready access may be obtained by a perpendicular railway, intersecting each story, in addition to the broad and capacious corridors and stairways, independent of the ordinary and usual approaches from floor to floor.

Hoffman House.

This is another elegant establishment, built of white marble, located on the corner of Broadway and Twenty-Fifth street, immediately opposite Madison Square. It is conducted on the European plan, and has excellent accommodations for about four hundred guests.

Its location is in the aristocratic portion of the city, and is central for all of the Eastern and Northern Railroads; forming a most convenient and delightful stopping place for travellers, while the beautiful grounds opposite render it an attrac-

ROTHHAN & CO.

MANUFACTURERS OF AND DEALERS IN

SADDLERY AND HARNESS,

323 BROADWAY, NEW YORK,
FACTORY, 202 MARKET ST., NEWARK, N. J.

I. L. ROTHHAN.   JOS. STRAUS.   ANDREW WILSON.

HOFFMAN HOUSE.
AND WORTH MONUMENT.

tive feature to all who have the pleasure of being its guests

Southern Hotel, formerly the Lafarge.

This popular house is situated on Broadway, opposite Bond street. It is constructed of white marble, with a frontage of two hundred feet, seven stories high, and completed in 1856 at a cost of $500,000. Has fine accommodations for six hundred guests.

The reputation of the Southern can be estimated by the fact that its "list" is always full. Those who may be so fortunate as to select this hotel during their residence in the city, will find its kind and courteous proprietor ever ready to contribute to their comfort and enjoyment.

New York Hotel

Is one of our oldest first-class houses. The building, located on the finest part of Broadway, extending from Washington to Waverly Place, is of brick, five stories high, with a front of five hundred feet. It is most commodiously and comfortably arranged for families and single persons, and is in the midst of elegant stores, and the most fashionable places of amusement. In its internal arrangements it is unsurpassed, and contains spacious accommodations for about four hundred guests. Messrs. Cranston & Hildreth are its proprietors, the former having been its worthy host for many years.

The Brevoort House,

On Fifth Avenue, corner of Eighth Street, is a noble and spacious Hotel, fitted up in elegant style, and being on the great avenue of fashion, commands a fine view of the *beau monde*. By a glance at the city map it will be seen that the central locality of this large and pleasant hotel secures a ready connection by railroad and stage with all the most desirable parts of the city from the Battery to Central Park.

The Everett House,

Located on the North side of Union Square and Seventeenth Street, from its position is a convenient and delightful place to stop, being not only in the aristocratic part of the city, but also contiguous to the Cars, Omnibuses, Places of Amusement, &c. The Everett has fine suites of apartments, as well as single rooms, with all the modern improvements and adornments of taste.

St. Denis Hotel.

Opposite Grace Church, and three blocks below Union Square, and the Academy of Music, is located the St. Denis. It is one among the very many handsome structures with which Broadway is lined, and occupies 76 feet on that thoroughfare and 120 feet on Eleventh Street. The Hotel is situated upon the most fashionable part of Broadway, and is the resort of the wealthy both of town and country. It contains over 150 large and handsome rooms, and is kept on the European plan. Meals served at all hours.

THE
Moseley Iron Bridge and Roof Co.
OFFICE, 116 WILLIAM STREET,
New York.

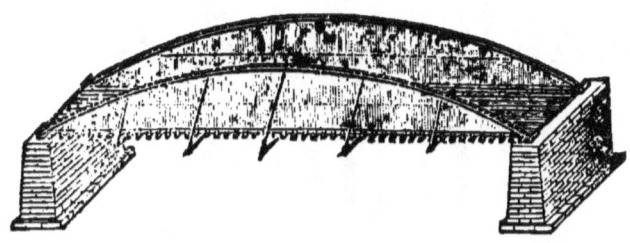

Are prepared to execute orders for the MOSELEY WROUGHT-IRON ARCH GIRDER BRIDGE, which is the most perfect combination of STRENGTH and LIGHTNESS of MATERIAL; and for SIMPLICITY, DURABILITY and CHEAPNESS is unequalled by any other BRIDGE in use for RAILROAD and HIGHWAY purposes. It has been adopted by the BOSTON, HARTFORD & ERIE and NEWARK & NEW YORK RAILROADS, and received the FIRST PREMIUM at the late FAIR of the AMERICAN INSTITUTE.

Also, IRON BUILDINGS for RAILROAD DEPOTS, MACHINE SHOPS, FACTORIES, CHURCHES, &c., and CORRUGATED SHEET-IRON for ROOFS, SIDING, FENCES, FLOORS, PARTITIONS, DOORS, SHUTTERS, &c. Models to be seen at our office. Circulars sent to applicants.

(*See page* 161.)

JAMES S. BARRON & CO.

Manufacturers and Wholesale Dealers in

MANILLA AND JUITE

ROPE,

CORDAGE, TWINES, WICKING,

Wooden and Willow Ware,

BROOMS, BRUSHES, ETC.

Mason's Blacking and Dixon's Stove Polish.

280 Washington Street,

(Between Warren and Chamber Streets,)

NEW YORK.

H. T. MODDRELL.

THE TOMBS.

Prescott House.
Spring street and Broadway, near St. Nicholas.

St. Denis,
Corner of Broadway and Eleventh street.
(European plan.)

Everett House,
Corner of Fourth avenue and Seventeenth street.

Clarendon,
Located corner of Fourth avenue and Eighteenth street.

Albemarle,
Situated corner of Broadway and Twenty-Fourth street.

St. James,
Corner of Fifth avenue and Twenty-Sixth street.

Brevoort House,
Fifth avenue, corner of Eighth street.

Gramercy Park House,
Situated on Gramercy Park Place, between Twentieth and Twenty-First streets, and Third and Fourth avenue.

Brandreth House.
(European plan.) Broadway and Canal street.

Irving House.
(European plan.) Broadway and Twelfth street.

Merchant's Hotel.
Is situated on Cortland street, near Greenwich.

Girard House.
West Broadway, corner Chambers street.

National Hotel.
Located on Cortland street, near Broadway.

Coleman House.
1169 Broadway, corner East Twenty-seventh street.

Western Hotel.
No. 13 Cortland street, near Broadway.

French's Hotel.
Corner of Chatham and Frankfort streets.

Earle's Hotel.
Corner Canal and Centre streets.

Westminster Hotel, (European Plan.)
Corner Irving Place and Sixteenth street.

Bancroft House.
906 Broadway.

MARKETS.

New York is not especially noted for its markets. There are quite a number of them, but none worthy of special notice. There is a large amount of business done in the

Washington Market,

Located on the square bounded by Fulton, Vesey, Washington and West streets. Here it is the produce from the Jersey shores and Long Island are offered for sale from the wagons of the farmer. In the spring of the year it is very interesting to see the large number of these wagons gathered about the streets contiguous to the market.

Fulton Market,

A poor, dilapidated concern, which occupies ground worth twenty times the value of the building, is situated on the square bounded by Fulton, Beekman, South and Front streets. This market, together with Washington Market, is nothing but a mere *shanty*, a disgrace to the city. A splendid illustration of the manner in which the "City Fathers" look after the welfare of this great metropolis.

Tompkins Market.

This market is the only one of any account, being a very fine iron structure, located on Third avenue, between Sixth and Seventh streets.

Clinton Market,
At the foot of Canal street, North River.

Jefferson Market,
Corner of Sixth and Greenwich avenues.

Catharine Market
Occupies a square between Cherry, South and Catharine streets.

Centre Market,
This building is partially of brick, located on Centre. extending from Grand to Broome streets.

Chelsea Market,
Ninth avenue, near Eighteenth street.

CEMETERIES.

The salutary effects of ornate and well-preserved cemeteries on the moral taste and general sentiments of all classes, are a most valuable result, and seem to have been appreciated in all ages by all civilized nations. The Etruscans, the Egyptians, the Greeks, the Romans, and in modern times the Turks, all illustrate not only their skill in the arts and their intellectual excellence, but also their social affections and refinements, and all the gentler characteristics, by a studied attention to cemeteries for the dead. If we seek for authority more commanding in its influence, we may look to the patriarchs of Israel, who manifested a spirit of reverence and solicitude for the

J.B. & W.W. CORNELL,
PLAIN & ORNAMENTAL
IRON WORKS,
135 to 143 CENTRE ST,
NEW YORK.

burial places of their dead, more enlightened, but not less active or pervading. Let us have the "field and the cave which is therein and all the trees which are in the field," and "that are in the borders round about, to be made sure for a possession of a burying-place." And there "Abraham buried Sarah his wife."

Greenwood Cemetery.

This beautiful resting-place of the dead is located on Long Island, about three miles from Fulton Ferry, or two and one half miles from South Ferry, from which points cars start for the cemetery direct every five minutes.

The cemetery contains about 400 acres, and is of undulating and varied character. The principal avenue is named The Tour, and by keeping this strangers will secure the most favorable general view. Attention is called to the guide-boards in the grounds, which will enable them more easily to tread their way through the retired but not less beautiful passages within this solemn enclosure. There are so many beautiful monuments, tombs and ornamental lots, that it is impossible to call special attention to any. Suffice it to say, that the surface of the earth anywhere in the same space does not contain so many memorials of such beauty and so varied in design, as are to be found placed over the remains of the 127,000 dead that have been laid at rest within this cemetery since 1838.

STEAMBOATS.

Albany (Morning),	Pier 39 North River.
" (Night)	" 41 "
Albany & Troy (Night),	" 44 "
Astoria,	" 24 East River.
Boston (Newport),	" 28 North River
Boston (Stonington),	" 18 "
Boston (Norwich),	" 39 "
Bergen Point,	" 26 "
Blackwell's Island,	61st East River
Bridgeport,	Pier 35 "
Bull's Ferry,	" 48 North River.
Cold Spring,	" 39 "
Catskill,	" 35 "
College Point,	" 22 East River.
Elm Park,	" 26 North River.
Elizabeth,	" 26 "
Fort Lee,	" 48 "
Flushing,	" 22 East River.
Glen Cove,	" 14 "
Greenwich,	" 38 "
Harlem,	" 24 "
Hartford,	" 24 "
Haverstraw,	" 34 North River,
High Bridge,	" 24 East River.
Hudson,	" 37 North River.
Kingston,	" 33 "
Keyport,	" 26 "
Long Branch,	" 32 "

Steamboats.—*Continued.*

Middletown Point,	Pier 26	North River.
New Brighton, L. I.,	" 19	"
New Haven,	" 25	East River.
Newark,	" 26	North River.
Newburgh,	" 39	"
Nyac,	" 34	"
Peekskill,	" 32	"
Perth Amboy,	" 1	"
Philadelphia,	" 1	"
Port Monmouth,	" 32	"
Poughkeepsie,	" 39	"
Providence,	" 35	"
Rockaway,	" 28	"
Rondout,	" 39	"
Red Bank,	" 32	"
Sailors' Long Harbor,	" 19	"
Shrewsbury,	" 26	"
Sing Sing,	" 34	"
Staten Island (north shore),	" 19	"
Staten Island (south shore),	Battery,	East River.
South Amboy,	Pier 1	North River.
Stamford,	" 22	East River.
Tarrytown,	" 34	North River.
West Point,	" 39	"
Yonkers,	" 34	"

☞ See page 135.

POLITENESS IN RAILROAD CARS.

The following Rules should be observed, to make travelling on Railroads comfortable:

1. Always show your ticket (without getting in a bad humor) whenever the conductor asks for it. Observe this rule, and it will *pay*.

2. A gentleman should not occupy more than one seat at a time.

3. *Gentlemen* will not spit tobacco juice in the cars where there are ladies; it soils their skirts and dresses.

4. *Ladies* without escort in travelling, should be very particular with whom they become acquainted.

5. "If your lips would save from slips,
   Five things observe with care:
Of whom you speak,—to whom you speak,—
   And how,—and when,—and where."

6. Whenever you see a fellow over-anxious for your comfort, and pushing himself forward, saying, "Are you travelling alone?—Allow me to," &c., &c.; just say to him, "Thank you, sir, I require no assistance." By observing this rule, ladies will often save themselves and others trouble.

7. Ladies travelling with children should invariably have a basket of eatables; a tumbler or goblet for the children to drink from, and keep the children in their seats.

8. Keep your head and arms inside the windows.

9. Never sit in a seat, in warm weather, with a man weighing 244 pounds.

10. Always carry greenbacks instead of individual promises to pay.

FREEMAN & BURR, CLOTHIERS

Merchant Tailors
AND
OUTFITTERS,
IN
Gentlemen's & Boys' Clothing
OF EVERY DESCRIPTION.
FURNISHING GOODS, &c.

THE
BEST FOREIGN & DOMESTIC FABRICS,
Always in Stock for Orders and to Measure.

FREEMAN & BURR,
No. 124 FULTON ST., and 90 NASSAU ST.,
(S. E. Corner Fulton and Nassau Sts.,)
NEW YORK.

CONTINENTAL
LIFE INSURANCE COMPANY,
OF NEW YORK.

Policies issued in 1867, · · · 4,188.
Amount insured " · · · $11,970,000.
Income in 1867, · · · · · $807,249.
Dividend declared Jan. 1868, 40 per ct.

OFFICE, No. 26 NASSAU STREET.

ORGANIZED ON THE MUTUAL PLAN.

PROFITS OF THE COMPANY
Annually Divided.

One-Third of the Premium may remain unpaid as a LOAN.
NO NOTES REQUIRED.   POLICIES NON-FORFEITABLE.
Thirty Days' Grace Allowed in Payment of Premiums.
Insured have the widest liberty to travel
Without Extra Charge.

$100,000 deposited with the State Superintendent of Insurance, at Albany, in compliance with the State Law.
Branch Offices established in most of the principal cities in the U. States.

OFFICERS.

JUSTUS LAWRENCE, ... President.
G. HILTON SCRIBNER, ... Vice-President.
J. P. ROGERS, ... Secretary.
R. C. FROST, ... Actuary.
E. D. WHEELER, M.D., ... Medical Examiner.

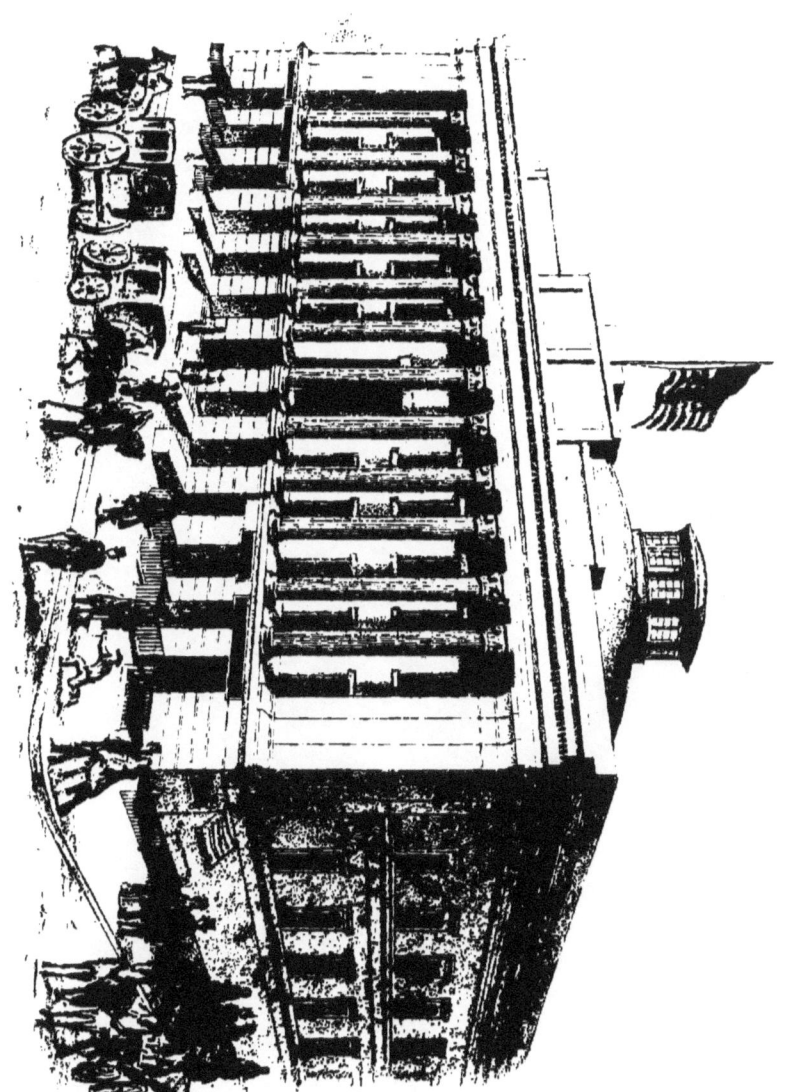

CUSTOM HOUSE.

11. Ladies who wear hoops should make them small before leaving home.

12. Never let your bandbox, valise or cloak occupy a seat, when there is a rack for them; it looks bad for you to occupy a whole seat when there are passengers standing without seats.

13. Always be polite to everybody while travelling; don't get in a bad humor.

14. Never give information without being asked, then you will not be contradicted.

15. When a lady enters the car, and there is no seat vacant, rise and proffer yours,—it is true politeness.

16. Never sit on the end of another person's seat with your back turned, talking to an opposite party;—it is disagreeable to the one whose seat you are thus obtruding yourself on.

17. Never smoke in a car where there are ladies—no gentleman would be guilty of such an act.

18. Never use profane language in a railroad car.

19. Never talk on politics in the cars;—it is usually disagreeable to some of your fellow travellers.

20. Never talk loud while the train is in motion; it may not annoy any one, but it will injure your lungs.

21. Never sit beside a person who is hard of hearing, and has never travelled any; get away, there are too many questions to be answered.

22. Making love should be done outside of railroad cars; by being too affectionate in the cars, people will talk.

RAILROADS.

Below will be found the location of the depots of the various railroads diverging from New York. For arrival and departure of trains the daily papers must be consulted; the changes with the seasons being so frequent as to preclude the possibility of affixing a permanent table here.

Hudson River Railroad Depot, Thirtieth street and Tenth avenue.

Erie Railroad Depot, foot Chamber street.

New Haven Railroad Depot, Twenty-seventh street and Fourth avenue.

Harlem Railroad Depot, Twenty-sixth street and Fourth avenue.

Long Island Railroad Depot, James' Slip and Thirty-fourth street, East River.

New Jersey Central Railroad Depot, foot of Liberty street.

Camden and Amboy Railroad Depot, Pier 1, Battery.

Morris and Essex Railroad Depot, foot Barclay street.

Northern Railroad of New Jersey, foot Courtland street.

Flushing Railroad, James Slip and Thirty-fourth street.

Raritan and Delaware Bay Railroad, foot of Duane street.

Staten Island Railroad, foot Whitehall street.

New Jersey Railroad, foot Courtland street.

BERKSHIRE
Life Insurance Company,
INCORPORATED 1851.

All Policies non-forfeitable.

CASH ASSETS, - - - - $1,000,000.

NEW YORK OFFICE,

271 BROADWAY.

I. HAMBURGER & CO.
IMPORTERS OF
PIPES,
SMOKER'S ARTICLES
AND
CUTLERY,

No. 55 Maiden Lane, & 385 Broadway,

New York

MAURICE WILKINSON.   GEORGE WILKINSON.

M. & G. WILKINSON,
WHOLESALE DEALERS IN
Wooden and Willow Ware,
BAGGING, ROPE, CORDAGE,

Brooms, Mats, Baskets, Twines, Matches, Blacking, Wrapping-Paper, &c.

242 CANAL STREET,
(Opposite Earle's Hotel,)

FRED'K WILKINSON,   New York.   SILAS C. AYRES,
Late Lathrop & Wilkinson.   *Late with H. G. Law & Bro.*

THE NEW KID GLOVE.

LAPORTE'S
PARIS KID GLOVES,
ARE THE BEST IN THE WORLD

The undersigned are Sole Agents in the United States for Laporte's entire manufacture of Kid and Dogskin Gloves in Men's and Women's sizes; and PATENTEES and MANUFACTURERS of the Celebrated **PATENT PANTALOON DRAWERS.**
Each pair of the genuine will bear this Trade-mark—

PATENTED FEBRUARY 4, 1868

Always on hand, a full line of our well-known
PARAGON SHIRTS
and a choice stock of MEN'S FURNISHING GOODS, adapted to the fine trade.

FISK, CLARK & FLAGG,
No. 58 White Street, New York.

(See page 122.)

ASTOR HOUSE

Hackensack and New York, foot Chamber st.
Brooklyn and Jamaica, South Ferry.
Perth Amboy and Woodbridge, foot Courtland street.
Long Branch and Sea Shore, Pier 26, N. River.

CITY RAILROADS.

To New York belongs the credit of having originated the now widely-extended system of City Railway travel. They have now become so extensive that almost any part of the city or suburbs may be reached without any inconvenience. The following roads are in operation:

First and Second Avenue Line.

From Peck Slip up Oliver, Bowery, Grand, Christie, First avenue, East Twenty-third street to Second avenue and Harlem. Return same route.

Third Avenue Line.

From Park Row up Chatham, Bowery, Third avenue to Harlem. Return same route.

Fourth Avenue Line.

From Park Row up Centre, Grand, Bowery, Fourth avenue to Thirtieth street. Return same route.

Sixth Avenue Line.

From Vesey st. and Broadway through Church, Chamber, West Broadway, Canal, Varick, Carmine and Sixth avenue to Fifty-ninth st. Return same route.

Seventh Avenue Line.

From Barclay and Broadway, through Church street, Green, University place, Broadway, Forty-third street and Seventh avenue to Fifty-ninth street. Returning same route.

There is a branch starting from corner of Broadway and Broome street.

Eighth Avenue Line.

From Vesey st. and Broadway, through Church, Chamber, West Broadway, Canal, Hudson and Eighth avenue to Fifty-ninth street. Return same route.

Ninth Avenue Line.

From Barclay street corner of Church, through Church, Chamber, West Broadway, Canal, Greenwich and Ninth avenue to Fifty-ninth st. Return same route.

Broadway and Grand Street Ferry Line.

From corner of Broadway and Canal street, through New Canal, East Broadway and Grand street to Grand street ferry. Return same route.

East Broadway and Dry Dock Line.

From Broadway and Park Row, through Chatham, East Broadway, Grand, Goerck, Houston to Avenue D, thence through Avenue D to Dry Dock.

Return route—From Dry Dock through Avenue D, Eighth, Lewis, Grand, East Broadway, Chatham and Park Row to Broadway.

Fulton Ferry, Bleecker and Fourteenth St. Line.

From Fulton Ferry through Fulton st., William, Ann, Park Row, Centre, Reade, Elm, Grand, Crosby, Bleecker, Hudson and West Fourteenth to North River.

Return same route, except from Park Row, down Beekman to South and Fulton Ferry.

Central Park, North and East River Railroad, Eastern Division.

From South ferry through Front, Water, South to Wall street ferry, Fulton ferry, Catharine ferry, Roosevelt street ferry, James' slip ferry to Grand street ferry; thence through Grand, Mangin, Corlears and Houston streets to Avenues D and A; thence through Fourteenth street to First avenue, and through First avenue and Fifty-ninth street to Fifth avenue. Return same route.

Central Park North and East River Railroad Line, Western Division.

From South ferry through Whitehall, Battery Place and West street to Jersey City and Hoboken ferries, thence through West street to Tenth avenue and Fifty-ninth street and Fifth avenue. Return same route.

Forty-Second and Grand St. Ferry Railroad Line

From Forty-second street and Eleventh avenue, along Forty-second st. to Tenth avenue, through Tenth avenue to Thirty-fourth street, Broadway, Twenty-third street, Fourth avenue, Fourteenth street, Avenue A, Houston street, Cannon, Grand to Grand street ferry.

Return route—From Grand st. ferry to Goerck, Houston, Second, Avenue A, Fourteenth, Fourth avenue, Twenty-third street, Broadway, Thirty-fourth, Tenth avenue to Forty-second street ferry.

Single fare on any of the line of cars six cents.

OMNIBUSES.

Fifth Avenue Line.

From Fulton ferry up Fulton street, Broadway Eleventh street, University Place, Fifth avenue to Forty-second. Return same route.

Madison Avenue Line.

From Wall street ferry up Wall, Broadway and Madison avenue to Twenty-third street. Return same route.

Broadway Line.

From South ferry up Broadway to Twenty-third street. Return same route.

Houston Street Line.

From South ferry up Broadway, Chatham,

BEEKMAN FIRE INSURANCE COMPANY
CASH CAPITAL $200,000
172 BROADWAY, NEW YORK, Corner MAIDEN LANE

INSURES AGAINST LOSS & DAMAGE BY FIRE

BENJAMIN W. BENSON
President

CHAS. H. ROSER, Sec'y   C. A. BETTS, Ass't Sec'y

DIRECTORS:

A. C. Kingsland.	Seely Brown.	Alex. Dalrymple.	Oliver H. Jones.
James Morrison.	Alpheus Underhill.	Henry S. Van Beuren.	John A. Van Blarcom.
Wright Gillies.	Thomas E. Cooper.	H. Birdenburgh.	Nathaniel Whitman.
M. M. Van Beuren.	David Jones.	Washington Yale.	Philip G. Weaver.
Ebenezer Collamore.	I. D. Condit.	John N. Eitel.	A. L. Sarre.
Albert Journeay.	H. M. Baldwin.	Thomas Davenport.	Henry Randel.
Jonathan Edgar.	George W. Todd.	James J. Winant.	Samuel Raynor.
J. O. Fowler.	William Adams.	Aaron Raymond.	Lucien B. Stone.
Daniel Hodgman.	David Close.	James W. Scribner.	F. W. Hutchins.
George J. Byrd.	William Van Nrone.	Gershom Banker.	Benjamin W. Benson.

Bowery, Houston to Houston street ferry. Return same route. Fare on omnibuses ten cents.

FERRY BOATS.

From South Ferry to Hamilton Avenue, Brooklyn.
" " Atlantic street, "
" Wall street to Montague street, "
" Fulton street to Fulton street, "
" Catharine street to Main street, "
" Grand street to Grand street, "
" Houston street to Grand street, "
" Roosevelt st. to South Seventh st., "
" Jackson street to Hudson avenue, "
" Courtland st. to Montgomery st., Jersey City
" Desbrosses st. to " " "
" Chamber street to Pavonia avenue, "
" Barclay street to Hoboken.
" Canal street to Hoboken.
" Christopher street to Hoboken,
" Dey street to (north side) Staten Island.
" Whitehall street to (south side) "
" Thirty-fourth street to Hunter's Point, L. I.
" James Slip to " "
" Tenth street, East River, to Green Point.
" Twenty-third st. " "
" Forty-second st. North River, to Wehawken.

LOCATION OF PIERS

EAST RIVER.

1, 2, foot Whitehall street.
3, foot Moore street.

10*

4, between Moore and Broad street.
5, between Broad and Coenties Slip.
6, 7, 8, Coenties Slip.
9, 10, between Coenties and Old Slip.
11, 12, Old Slip.
13, between Old Slip and Gouverneur's Lane.
14, foot Jones' Lane.
15, 16, foot Wall street.
17, foot Pine street.
18, foot Maiden Lane.
19, foot Fletcher street.
20, 21, foot Burling Slip.
22, foot Fulton street.
23, foot Beekman street.
24, between Beekman street and Peck Slip.
25, 26, Peck Slip.
27, foot Dover street.
28, between Dover and Roosevelt streets.
29, foot Roosevelt street.
30, between Roosevelt and James street.
31, 32, James' Slip.
33, foot Oliver street.
34, 35, foot Catharine street.
36, 37, foot Market street.
38, between Market street and Pike Slip.
39, 40, foot Pike street.
41, between Pike and Rutger street.
42, 43, foot Rutger street.
44, foot Jefferson street.
45, foot Clinton street.
46, between Clinton and Montgomery street.

FREEMAN & BURR, CLOTHIERS

Merchant Tailors

AND

OUTFITTERS,

IN

Gentlemen's & Boys' Clothing

OF EVERY DESCRIPTION.

FURNISHING GOODS, &C.

THE
BEST FOREIGN & DOMESTIC FABRICS,
Always in Stock for Orders and to Measure.

FREEMAN & BURR,

No. 124 FULTON ST., and 90 NASSAU ST.,

(S. E. Corner Fulton and Nassau Sts.,)

NEW YORK.

C. F. A. HINRICHS,

(Successor to M. WERCKMEISTER.
Established 1801.)

Importer of and Dealer in

GLASS, CHINA,

Terra Cotta and Lava Ware,

GERMAN, FRENCH AND ENGLISH

FANCY GOODS,

SMOKERS' ARTICLES,

GAMES AND TOYS

OF ALL DESCRIPTIONS.

SOLE AGENT for the United States and Canada for the Glass Factories of the Compagnie Anonyme Namuroise, at Namur, Belgium.

Sole Agent for the United States and the whole of North and South America, for

C. A. KLEEMAN'S

Patent Student or St. Germain

LAMP.

Sole Agent for

HOCHAPFEL FRERES'

PATENT SMOKING-PIPES.

150 Broadway
AND
71 LIBERTY STREET,
116   NEW YORK.

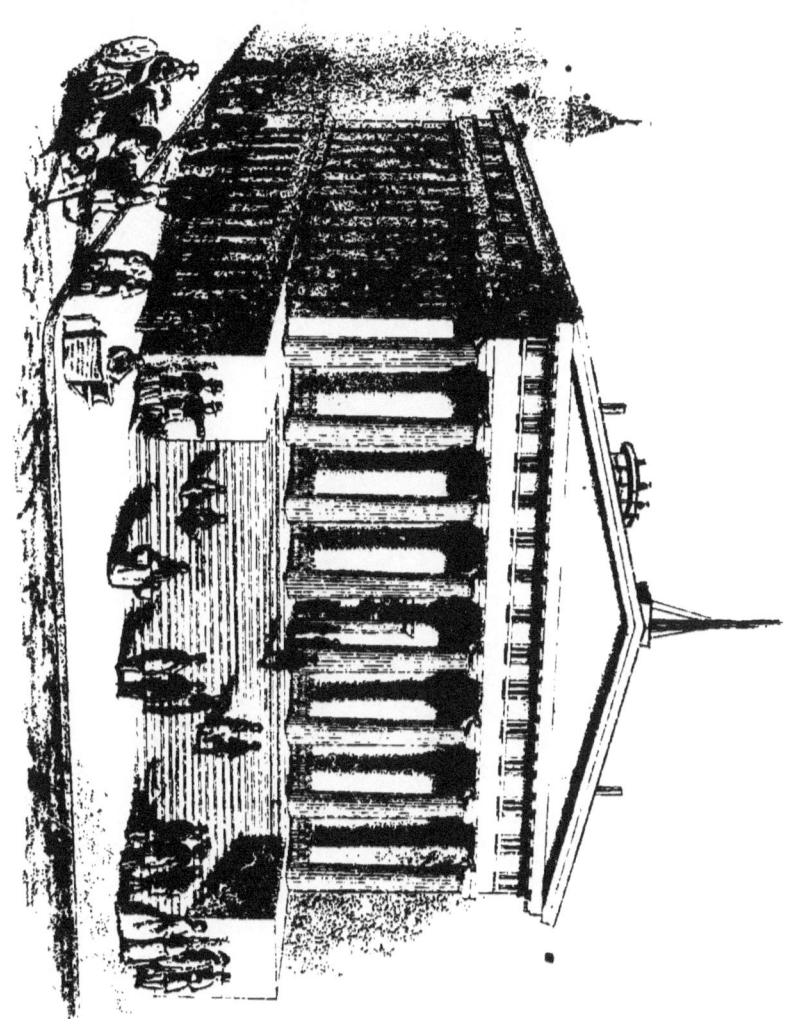
SUB TREASURY.

47, foot Montgomery street.
48, between Montgomery and Gouverneur Slip.
49, Gouverneur Slip.
50, between Gouverneur Slip and Walnut street.
51, 52, foot Walnut street.
53, 54, foot Grand street.
55, 56, foot Broome street.
57, foot Delancy streets.
58, between Rivington and Stanton streets.

North River.

1, foot Battery Place.
2, 3, between Battery Place and Morris street.
4, foot Morris street.
5, 6, between Morris and Rector streets.
7, foot Rector street.
8, between Rector and Carlisle streets.
9, foot Carlisle street.
10, foot Albany street.
11, between Albany and Cedar streets.
12, foot Cedar street.
13, foot Liberty street.
14, between Liberty and Courtland streets.
15, 16, foot Courtland street.
17, between Courtland and Dey streets.
18, foot Dey street.
19, foot Fulton street.
20, between Fulton and Vesey streets.
21, foot Vesey street.
22, between Vesey and Barclay streets.
23, 24, foot Barclay street.

25, foot Robinson street.
26, foot Murray street.
27, foot Warren street.
28, foot Chamber street.
29, foot Duane street.
30, between Duane and Jay streets.
31, foot Jay street.
32, foot Harrison street.
33, foot Franklin street.
34, foot North Moore street.
35, foot Beach street.
36, foot Hubert street.
37, foot Vestry street.
37½, foot Desbrosses street.
38, foot Watts street.
39, 40, foot Canal street.
41, foot Spring street.
42, between Spring and Charlton streets.
43, foot Charlton street.
44, foot King street.
45, foot Hamersley street.
46, foot Clarkson street.
47, foot Morton street.
48, foot Christopher street.
49, foot Amos street.
50, foot Charles street.
51, foot Perry street.
52, foot Hammond street.
53, foot Bank street.
54, foot Troy street.

HACK FARES.

One passenger, not exceeding one mile,	$0 50
Two passengers, not exceeding one mile,	75
Every additional passenger,	37½
Every passenger, exceeding one mile and within two miles,	75
Every additional passenger,	37½
Use of a hackney-coach by the day, with one or more passengers,	5 00
Use of a hackney-coach by the hour, with privilege of going from place to place and stopping as often as required,	1 00

When the hiring of a hackney-coach is **not**, at the time, specified to be by the day or **hour**, it shall be deemed by the mile.

Children between two and fourteen years of age, half price; under two years, no charge.

Every passenger shall be allowed one trunk, valise, saddle-bag, carpet-bag, or box, as baggage; for every additional article named, six cents.

The number shall be placed on each carriage or coach, and the license and tariff of rates posted therein.

In case of infringement as to price or distance, passengers will report to the Mayor, at the City Hall for redress.

TABLE OF DISTANCES.

From the Battery.	From the Exchange.	From City Hall.	To
½ of a mile.	¼ of a mile.	....	Fulton street.
¾ "	½ "	....	Warren "
1 "	¾ "	¼ of a mile.	Leonard "
1¼ "	1 mile.	½ "	Canal "
1½ "	1¼ "	¾ "	Spring "
1¾ "	1½ "	1 mile.	Houston "
2 "	1¾ "	1¼ "	4th "
2¼ "	2 "	1½ "	9th "
2½ "	2¼ "	1¾ "	14th "
2¾ "	2½ "	2 "	17th "
3 "	2¾ "	2¼ "	24th "
3¼ "	3 "	2½ "	29th "
3½ "	3¼ "	2¾ "	34th "
3¾ "	3½ "	3 "	38th "
4 "	3¾ "	3¼ "	44th "
4¼ "	4 "	3½ "	49th "
4½ "	4¼ "	3¾ "	54th "
4¾ "	4½ "	4 "	58th "
5 "	4¾ "	4¼ "	63d "
5¼ "	5 "	4½ "	68th "
5½ "	5¼ "	4¾ "	73d "
5¾ "	5½ "	5 "	78th "
6 "	5¾ "	5¼ "	83d "
6¼ "	6 "	5½ "	88th "
6½ "	6¼ "	5¾ "	93d "
6¾ "	6½ "	6 "	97th "
7 "	6¾ "	6¼ "	102d "
7¼ "	7 "	6½ "	107th "
7½ "	7¼ "	6¾ "	112th "
7¾ "	7½ "	7 "	117th "
8 "	7¾ "	7¼ "	121st "
8¼ "	8 "	7½ "	126th "
8½ "	8¼ "	7¾ "	131st "
8¾ "	8½ "	8 "	156th "
9 "	8¾ "	8¼ "	140th "
9¼ "	9 "	8½ "	145th "
9½ "	9¼ "	8¾ "	150th "
9¾ "	9½ "	9 "	154th "

MERRILL & CO.
47 WALKER STREET,
New York.

4 Washington Street, Chicago.

IMPORTERS AND JOBBERS OF

Clothiers' and Tailors'
TRIMMINGS,
BUTTONS
IN EVERY STYLE AND VARIETY.

BRAIDS AND BINDINGS
IN ALL QUALITIES AND KINDS.

SEWING-SILKS,
MACHINE-TWIST,
BUTTON-HOLE TWIST.

Our Silks and Twists are unsurpassed in quality, and we sell as low as any manufacturer.

HAIR-CLOTHS, BUCKLES, CRAYONS, &c., &c.

We have also added to our stock a full line of

PIECE TRIMMINGS.

THE NEW KID GLOVE.

LAPORTE'S
PARIS KID GLOVES,
ARE THE BEST IN THE WORLD!

The undersigned are Sole Agents in the United States for Laporte's entire manufacture of Kid and Dogskin Gloves in Men's and Women's sizes; and PATENTEES and MANUFACTURERS of the Celebrated **PATENT PANTALOON DRAWERS.**
Each pair of the genuine will bear this Trade-mark—

PATENTED FEBRUARY 4, 1868.

Always on hand, a full line of our well-known
PARAGON SHIRTS
and a choice stock of MEN'S FURNISHING GOODS, adapted to th fine trade.

FISK, CLARK & FLAGG,
No. 58 White Street, New York.

(See page 108.)

METROPOLITAN HOTEL.

POLICE STATIONS.

PRECINCT.	STREET.
First	54 New.
Second	49 Beckman.
Third	160 Chamber.
Fourth	9 Oak.
Fifth	49 Leonard.
Sixth	9 Franklin.
Seventh	247 Madison.
Eighth	126 Wooster.
Ninth	94 Charles.
Tenth	Essex Market.
Eleventh	Union "
Twelfth	126th street, near 3d avenue.
Thirteenth	Attorney st., near Delancy.
Fourteenth	53 Spring.
Fifteenth	221 Mercer.
Sixteenth	156 West Twentieth.
Seventeenth	1st avenue, cor. Fifth st.
Eighteenth	165 East Twenty-second.
Nineteenth	118 East Fifty-ninth.
Twentieth	325 West Thirty-fifth.
Twenty-first	120 East Thirty-fifth.
Twenty-second	545 West Forty-seventh.
Twenty-third	East 86th street, near 4th av.
Twenty-fourth	Whitehall, corner State.
Twenth-fifth	300 Mulberry.
Twenty-sixth	City Hall.
Twenty-seventh	99 Liberty.
Twenty-eighth	550 Greenwich.
Twenty-ninth	34 East Twenty-ninth.
Thirtieth	135th st., Manhattanville.
Thirty-first	86th st., Bloomingdale.
Thirty-second	152d st. and 10th avenue.

RAILROAD DISTANCES.

For the convenience of travellers, we append a table of distances from New York to the principal cities, and places of summer resort, in the United States.

New York to		New York to	
Albany, N. Y.	144	Mobile, Ala.	1431
Augusta, Ga.	891	Memphis, Tenn.	1586
Atlanta, Ga.	1062	Montreal, Canada.	403
Baltimore, Md.	187	New Haven, Ct.	76
Boston, Mass.	230	New Orleans, La.	1597
Buffalo, N. Y.	423	Pittsburg, Pa.	440
Burlington, Vt.	300	Portland, Me.	336
Cleveland, Ohio.	602	Providence, R. I.	188
Columbus, Ohio.	714	Petersburg, Va.	380
Cincinnati, Ohio.	807	Philadelphia, Pa.	90
Chicago, Ill.	908	Quebec, Canada.	583
Canandaigua, N.Y.	349	Reading, Pa.	148
Charleston, S. C.	782	Richmond, Va.	358
Detroit, Mich.	665	Rochester, N. Y.	373
Elmira, N. Y.	274	Savannah, Ga.	907
Fort Wayne, Ind.	698	Springfield, Mass.	138
Harrisburg, Pa.	179	St. Paul, Minn.	1463
Hartford, Ct.	102	St. Louis, Mo.	1151
Indianapolis, Ind.	838	Toledo, Ohio.	703
Louisville, Ky.	940	Williamsport, Pa.	285
Lynchburg, Va.	479	Wilmington, N. C.	605
Milwaukie, Wis.	1047	Washington, D. C.	227
Macon, Ga.	1051	Worceste Mass.	181

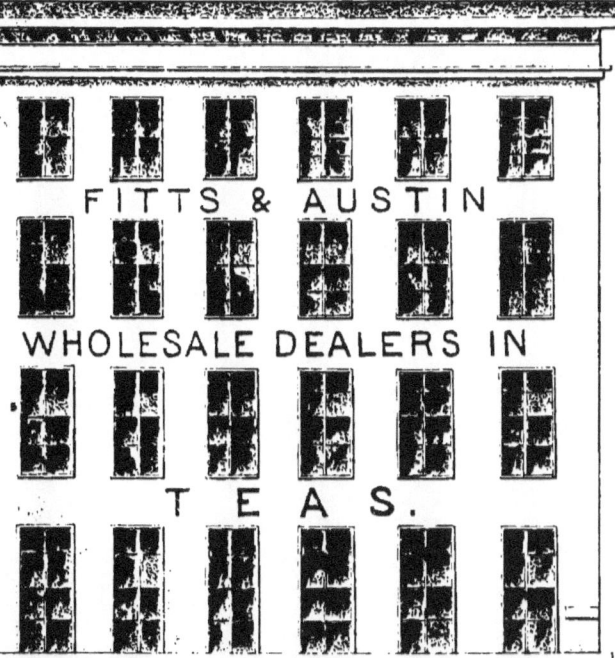

WATERING PLACES, ETC.

New York to

Avon Springs, N. Y.	391
Atlantic City, N. J.	100
Bedford Springs, Pa.	340
Cape May, N. J.	129
Columbia Springs, N. Y.	120
Catskill Mountains, N. Y.	111
Clarendon Springs, Vt.	240
Delaware Water Gap, Pa.	97
Lebanon Springs, N. Y.	183
Lake George, N. Y.	216
" Champlain, N. Y.	230
" Mahopac, N. Y.	56
" Memphremagog, Vt.	304
Long Branch, N. J.	32
Mount Vernon, Va.	242
Mount Holyoke, Mass.	155
Mammoth Cave, Ky.	959
Newport, R. I.	144
Niagara Falls, N. Y.	449
Natural Bridge, Va.	421
Sharon Spring, N. Y.	264
Saratoga Springs, N. Y.	183
Trenton Falls, N. Y.	256
White Mountains, N. H.	320
West Point, N. Y.	52
White Sulphur Springs, Va.	364

11*

GUIDE

TO THE

HUDSON RIVER

AND

Lake George:

COMPRISING NOTICES OF

EVERY OBJECT OF INTEREST TO STRANGERS.

WITH

Map and Numerous Illustrations.

NEW YORK AND PHILADELPHIA
ORNAMENTAL
IRON AND TERRA COTTA WORKS.

GARDEN AND CEMETERY ADORNMENTS,
IN IRON AND TERRA COTTA.

Fountains, Vases, Statuary, Summer-Houses, Arbors, Chairs, Settees, &c. Wire Trellises and Arches, for Vines, Flowers, &c.

IRON FURNITURE,
BEDSTEADS

Of every description, for Dwellings, Public Institutions, Hospitals, Prisons, &c.

PATENT SPRING BEDS, MATTRESSES, &c.

STABLE FIXTURES,
HAY RACKS, MANGERS, STALL DIVISIONS, ETC.

☞ Improved Composition Iron Railing ☜
OF WROUGHT AND CAST IRON COMBINED,

For inclosing Cemetery Plots, Offices, Dwellings, Public Squares, &c.

The Best, Strongest, and Cheapest Railing ever manufactured.

☞ Having purchased in March, 1864, the entire stock of Iron Goods of the New York Wire Railing Company, HUTCHINSON and WICKERSHAM, late Agents, together with the Patent and all the Machinery, for the exclusive Manufacture of Crimped Wire Railing, Window Guards, Farm Fencing, &c., we still continue the manufacture of the same, in larger variety, and at greatly Reduced Prices.

CHASE & CO.
WAREROOMS, 524 BROADWAY,
(Opposite St. Nicholas Hotel,)

New York.

VE. J. MAGNIN, GUÉDIN & CO.

IMPORTERS OF

WATCHES,

JEWELRY,

Musical Boxes,

FANCY GOODS,

Clocks, Bronzes, &c.

14 Grand Quai,   2 Maiden Lane,
GENEVA, Switz'd.   **NEW YORK.**

Sole Agents for the NARDIN WATCH.

TOUR OF THE HUDSON.

It is fortunate, for the gratification and the cultivation of the public taste for the sublime and beautiful in natural scenery, when our great highways of travel chance to lead through such wondrous landscape as does the journey up the Hudson River from New York to Troy. Even to the wearied or hurried traveller this voyage is ever one of pleasure, in its unique and constantly varying attractions; its thousand associations—legendary, historical, poetical and social.

Every possible facility is now at command for the passage of the Hudson, either by the steamer or by railway, morning, noon, and night. The commercial traveller, thinking more of his destination than of the pleasures by the way, will take the Hudson River Railroad, which lies on the eastern bank of the river, kissing its waters continually, and ever and anon crossing wide bays and the mouths of tributary streams. The pleasure-seeking tourist, in quest of the picturesque, and with time to enjoy it, will assuredly go by water.

Hudson River.

This noble river, styled the Rhine of America, on account of its bold and picturesque scenery, was named after its discoverer, Hendrick Hudson. In the fall of 1607 this Dutch navigator, with his barque, the Half Moon, might have been seen ascending its waters until he reached Albany. Its source is in the mountain regions of the Adirondacks. Its entire extent is about three hundred miles; its navigable length, from New York to Troy, is one hundred and fifty miles.

To the Hudson belongs the honor, not only of possessing the finest river steamers in the world, but of *having borne upon its waters the first steamboat which ever floated*, when Robert Fulton ascended the river in the Clermont, in 1807, just two centuries after the first voyage of Hendrick Hudson, in his good barque the Half Moon.

There is very much of especial interest and attraction to the traveller making a tour of the Hudson. Its waters are vocal with the hallowed reminiscences of our Revolutionary struggle, and along its banks linger memories of the noble and heroic deeds of our forefathers; its rocks and valleys are chronicled with the blood of the martyrs of freedom. To make the journey as interesting and instructive as possible, we will note the leading towns and more important objects of interest.

Supposing that we are accompanying the pleasure-seeker, and therefore have taken passage in one of the "floating palaces" which leave New York in the morning (which enables us to have a view of both sides of the river), we will first direct our attention to the

Elysian Fields of Hoboken,

On the western side, together with the preci-

THE GREATEST NOVELTY OF THE AGE!

THE UNIVERSAL FAVORITE

OR IMPROVED

HANCOCK SEWING-MACHINE.

Patented August 6, 1867.

THE SIMPLEST,

BEST AND CHEAPEST MACHINE IN THE WORLD.

PRICE ONLY $5.00.

The need has long been felt of a Sewing-Machine that, while it should combine within itself the elements of beauty, simplicity, efficiency, and durability, should yet be sold at such a price as would place it within the reach of all.

In the "UNIVERSAL FAVORITE," we present such a machine to the public,—confident that all who purchase will find it to meet every reasonable expectation. It requires no recommendation from us; for wherever seen, its merits are instantly appreciated. It is established already as the "Ladies' Indispensable Companion," the "Poor Workingwoman's Friend," and the "Children's Special Institution;" while the cost — the important element in these days of high prices — is merely nominal.

If it possesses no other merit, it is unequalled as a beautiful, useful, and appropriate gift for a little girl. Each machine is perfectly adjusted and packed in a small box, with full and complete instructions how to use it. Orders per mail, accompanied with the above amount, will have prompt attention, and can be forwarded per Express at trifling cost, to any place in the country.

Please call and examine the Machine, now on exhibition and for sale by

CHASE & CO.
524 BROADWAY,
(Opposite St. Nicholas Hotel,)

NEW YORK.

FISH AND PROVISIONS.

Wholesale buyers will find our stock unequalled in quality, variety, and cheapness.

GEO. C. PARKER & BRO.

257 Washington Street,

(Corner of Murray,)

NEW YORK.

Mackerel,	Shoulders,	Saleratus,
Codfish,	Beef,	Cream Tartar,
Pollock,	Tongues,	Mustard,
Shad,	Lard,	Beans,
Whitefish,	Butter,	Peas,
Bluefish,	Cheese,	Dried Fruit,
Salmon,	Vinegar,	Blacking,
Herring,	Salt,	Stove-Polish,
Halibut,	Snuff,	Starch,
Pork,	Soap,	Paper,
Hams,	Candles,	Twine.

Extra Refined Kerosene.

JOHN L. PARKER.

pices of Weehawken, with its grave and memories of the unfortunate Alexander Hamilton, who fell in the duel with Burr.

The Palisades

Next claim our attention. These grand bluffs, rising to the height of five hundred feet, follow in an unbroken line for a distance of twenty miles. The rock is trap, columnar in formation, like the famous Giants' Causeway in Ireland.

Fort Lee.

Ten miles up the river and opposite One Hundred and Sixtieth street, New York. Some interesting memories of the Revolution are awakened here. The anxious thoughts of Washington turned to this point during that eventful period. A large force of Americans, in retreating from Fort Lee, were overpowered, and either slain or taken prisoners by a superior force of Hessian troops.

Fort Washington,

Another spot of deep historical interest, lies opposite, on the eastern side. It fell into the hands of the British, November 16, 1776, and the garrison of 3,000 men became prisoners of war. Fort Washington is situated upon the highest part of Manhattan Island, between One Hundred and Eighty-first and One Hundred and Eighty-sixth streets.

Yonkers,

Seventeen miles up the river, eastern side, is a beautiful and picturesque spot, with its magnificent villas. In 1777 a naval action occurred in front of Yonkers, between the American and British forces.

Fonthill.

This " castle," which formerly belonged to Edwin Forrest, is just below Yonkers, and is now owned and occupied by the Roman Catholic school of Mount St. Vincent.

Hastings,

Twenty miles from New York, on the eastern side, is a pleasant little village, in great favor with the citizens of New York, who eagerly seek homes amid its pleasant places.

Dobb's Ferry,

Two miles beyond, and still upon the eastern bank of the river, is an ancient settlement. It derives its name from that of an old family, which once possessed the region and established a ferry. Remains of Revolutionary times still exist here.

Irvington and "Sunny Side."

This beautiful village, twenty-five miles from New York, is named after Washington Irving,

P. A. DAILEY & CO.

298 Broadway,
(Up-stairs,)

New York.

IMPORTERS AND DEALERS IN

Cloths, Cassimeres, Alpacas,

CLOTHIERS' AND TAILORS'

TRIMMINGS, ETC.

Furriers' and Clothiers' Wadding
on Commission.

Italian Cloths a Specialty.

We buy for Cash, Job lots, Auction lots, and at private sale large lots of Woollens, &c., and can always offer bargains to the trade.

"Goods well bought are half sold."

whose unique little cottage, called *Sunnyside*, is close by upon the river bank, concealed from the view of the traveller by the dense growth of the surrounding trees and shrubbery.

Piermont,

Opposite, on the western bank of the river, is the outgrowth of the Erie Railroad, which place was formerly its grand terminus. The river here is three miles wide, and the shores, particularly upon the west, are so varied and bold as to present pleasing and attractive pictures.

Three miles back of Piermont is the town of Tappan, interesting as having been the headquarters of Washington during the Revolution, and as the spot, also, where Major Andre was imprisoned and executed. The house of the commander-in-chief and the jail of the ill-fated officer are still in good preservation. The spot where Andre was executed (October 2, 1780) is a short distance from the jail, which is now occupied as a tavern, under the title of the "'76 Stone House."

Nyac

Is the next village above Piermont, on the same side of the river. Red sandstone is quarried here in great quantities.

Tarrytown.

A very prosperous place, situated on the eastern shore, twenty-seven miles from New York. During the Revolution Tarrytown witnessed many stormy fights between marauding bands of both British and Americans. It was upon a spot near the village that Major Andre was arrested while returning to the British lines, after a visit to General Arnold. A simple monument, an obelisk of granite, indicates the place.

Sing Sing,

On the right, or western bank of the river, thirty-three miles from New York, from its elevated position, presents an imposing aspect. The State Prison is located about three-quarters of a mile below the village, and is in full view from the river. The buildings are large structures, erected by the convicts themselves, with material from the marble and limestone quarries which abound here. The main edifice is four hundred and eighty-four feet long, forty-four feet wide, and five stories high, with cells for one thousand occupants. The whole area occupied by the establishment is one hundred and thirty acres of ground.

The Croton enters the Hudson two miles above the village, where its artificial passage to the City of New York is begun.

Haverstraw,

Thirty-six miles up, is on the west side of the river. The manufacture of brick is carried on very extensively in this vicinity. We now touch upon sacred ground, as we re-enter amidst the

RICHARD GREEN,

IMPORTER OF

Hosiery, Gloves,

UNDERWEAR,

AND

FURNISHING GOODS

FOR

Ladies, Gentlemen, and Children.

779 BROADWAY;

(Between 9th and 10th Streets.)

FAMILIES visiting New York will find at our establishment the most complete assortment of the above goods from the first Manufactories of England, France, and Germany, at prices lower than ever before offered.

SHIRTS AND COLLARS
For Gentlemen and Boys

made to order in the most superior manner at short notice, and a perfect fit guaranteed in every instance.

An examination of our stock respectfully solicited.

☞ The One Price System strictly adhered to.

779 Broadway,

Between 9th and 10th Streets.

ESTABLISHED 1850.

scenes of our Revolutionary history, for in this vicinity is the famous battle-ground of

Stony Point.

The old light-house here, placed amidst the remains of the ancient fort, calls this scene to the notice of all passers. This fort fell into the hands of the enemy June 1, 1779. The Americans, however, determined to regain their lost possession. General Wayne, who commanded the proposed assault, is reported to have said to General Washington, "General, I'll storm hell, if you will only plan it." He did storm Stony Point, on the night of July 15th, 1779, and the next day he wrote to his commander that the fort and garrison were his.

Peekskill.

We now enter upon the commencement of the magnificent scenery of the Highlands. On the opposite or western side of the river looms up the rugged front of the Dunderburg Mountain, with other grand cliffs and precipices.

The village of Peekskill on the right, forty-three miles from New York, was named after John Peek, one of the early Dutch navigators, who mistook the creek, which comes into the river just above, for the continuation of the Hudson itself, and thus thinking himself at the end of his journey, ran his craft ashore and commenced his settlement.

Caldwell's Landing,

At the foot of Dunderburg Mountain, is memorable for the search so seriously and actively made for the private treasure which the famous Captain Kidd is said to have secreted at the bottom of the river here.

The Highlands.

This grand mountain group through which the Hudson now makes its way, extends over an area of about twenty-five miles. The landscape which these noble heights present, is of unrivalled magnificence and beauty. Passing round the point of Dunderburg, we see the small but picturesque Buttermilk Falls, on the west side. In the heart of the Highland Pass, and just below West Point on the west side, is

Cozzens,

A spacious and elegant summer hotel, which comes most beautifully into the pictures of the vicinage.

West Point,

From the unrivalled charms of its scenery, and its position as the seat of the largest military school in the United States, is one of the most charming spots on the Hudson. It is replete with interest too, as the centre of the important interests and incidents connected with the days of the Revolution. The Military Academy is in full

JOHN MUNROE & CO.

American Bankers,

No. 7 RUE SCRIBE, PARIS,

AND

No. 8 WALL STREET, NEW YORK.

Issue Circular Letters of Credit for Travellers in all parts of Europe, &c.

ALSO,

Commercial Credits.

view, occupying a noble plateau, 188 feet above the river. The remains of the old forts, Putnam and Clinton, together with the little glen called "Kosciusko's Garden," embellished with an obelisk erected to the memory of the noble Pole, are to be seen a short distance above the Academy. Near the steamboat landing may be seen the rock from which a chain was thrown across the river during the Revolution, to prevent the passage of the British vessels.

West Point, in the Revolution, was the great key of the river, which Arnold, then in command of the fort, would have betrayed into the possession of the enemy, but for the providential arrest of his co-plotter Andre, at Tarrytown below. The Military Academy was established by Congress in 1802, and is supported and controlled by the Government. West Point is fifty-two miles from New York.

Cold Spring and "Undercliff,"

Which now command our attention, are little above, on the eastern side of the river. The West Point Iron Foundry is located here. Undercliff was the residence for many years of the late general and poet George P. Morris. It is scarcely possible to find a spot of sweeter natural attractions than the site of Undercliff.

Cornwall and "Idlewild,"

On the west side, come first to our reach.

Cornwall is a rugged and picturesque little place, on the lofty Highland terrace. "Idlewild," the romantic home of N. P. Willis, is a little north of the village. In its multiplicity of charms, it is a retreat which any poet might be content to enjoy.

New Windsor,

On the western bank, just above Cornwall, is a place of historical interest. General Washington established his head-quarters here in 1779, and again in 1780.

Fishkill,

On the eastern side of the river, sixty-one miles from New York, is a pleasant little village. The old village of Fishkill is situated about three miles east of the landing. Two miles northeast of the landing is the Verplanck House, interesting as having once been the head-quarters of the Baron Steuben, and the place in which the famous *Society of the Cincinnati* was organized, in 1783.

On the opposite side of the river is

Newburgh,

Noted also as the head-quarters of General Washington. The house which he occupied is the boast of the town. It is in full view from the river, situated a little below the village. It was here that the Revolutionary Army was finally disbanded at the close of the war, June 23d, 1783.

(See page 11.)

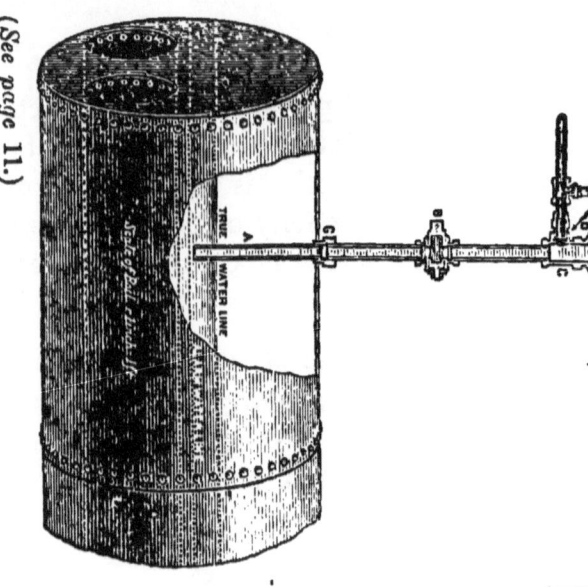

ASHCROFT'S
LOW WATER DETECTOR

Insures your Boiler against

EXPLOSION.

More than 8000 of them are in daily use.

Railway and Engineers' Supplies.

Send for Circular.

JOHN ASHCROFT,
50 John Street,
𝔑𝔢𝔴 𝔜𝔬𝔯𝔨.

New Hamburg

Comes next, on the eastern side. A little town, near the mouth of Wappinger's Creek. A tunnel, 1000 feet in length, through which the cars of the Hudson River Railroad pass, is to be seen just above the station.

Po'keepsie

Is seventy-five miles from New York, and the largest town between New York and Albany. It is built upon an eminence on the eastern side of the river. Settled by the Dutch in 1700. Professor Morse, of electric telegraph fame, and Benson J. Lossing, the historian, reside here.

New Paltz,

On the opposite side of the river, west, is a straggling little hamlet, of no special attraction.

Hyde Park.

This quiet little village, on the east side of the river, eighty miles from New York, is situated in the midst of a country of great fertility, and thronged with beautiful homesteads and sumptuous villas.

Rondout,

On the western side, one mile from the river, on Rondout Creek. The Delaware and Hudson Canal terminates here. The Rondout Creek is a singularly picturesque stream.

Kingston.

This town is situated (western side) on an elevated plain, three miles from the river. It was settled in 1663 by the Dutch. In the times of the Revolution it was burnt by the British. The first Constitution of the State of New York was framed and adopted in a house still standing at this place.

Rhinebeck

Is on the opposite side of the river and connected with Kingston by a ferry. Barrytown and Tivoli are small towns, on the east, above.

Saugerties

Is a handsome little village, on the west, at the debouchure of the beautiful waters of Æsopus Creek. We now pass Malden, on the left, and Germantown, on the right, and come to Oak Hill, a station on the railway for the opposite town of

Catskill,

At the mouth of the Catskill Creek, on the west side of the river. The village, which is a pleasant and thriving one, rises from the margin of the creek to an elevated site on the north, where it is dissipated in many beautiful country villas. Catskill is chiefly interesting to the tourist, as the point of detour towards the mountain ranges which lie over the valley, twelve miles westward. The Mountain House, upon the brink of a rocky ledge, two thousand and seven hundred feet

H. J. CIPPERLY & CO.

Manufacturers and Wholesale Dealers in

Straw Goods,

HATS, CAPS, FURS,

UMBRELLAS and PARASOLS,

250 & 252 Canal Street,

(Opposite Earle's Hotel,)

NEW YORK.

H. J. CIPPERLY.   P. H. MALLOY.   R. W. SMITH.

above the river, is in full view. In its pictorial attractions this is one of the most delightful points of our present tour, and we can commend to the traveller no pleasanter or more profitable summer excursion, for a day, or a month, than a visit to the Catskills, one of the grandest and most picturesque of the mountain ranges of the United States.

Hudson,

On the eastern side, one hundred and sixteen miles from New York, is one of the most important river towns. Just above the landing a bold promontory rises eighty feet above the river, upon which there is a beautiful park. Hudson is the chief terminus of the Boston and Hudson Railway. Passengers for the Shaker village, at New Lebanon, and Lebanon Springs, thirty-six miles distant, by the Hudson and Berkshire Road, and the Columbia Springs, only five miles distant, stop here.

Athens, on the west, and Stockport, Coxsackie, and Stuyvesant, on the east, are thriving little towns.

Kinderhook.

The village is situated five miles east of the landing, on the east side of the river. Here the late Martin Van Buren was born and died. His residence, "Lindenwold," is two miles south of the village. New Baltimore, and Coyeman's, on the west, Schodack, Castleton, and Greenbrush, on the east, brings us to

Albany,

The capital of the State, on the west. Albany was founded by the Dutch in 1614. It has a population of about eighty thousand. It is the great *entrepot* of the Erie Canal, from the west, and Champlain Canal, from the north, and is the centre of many lines of travel. The Dudley Observatory, located here, together with its public institutions, make it an interesting stopping-place for the tourist. Travellers for Sharon Springs will take the New York Central Railroad here, stopping at Palatine Bridge, fifty-five miles from Albany. For Richfield Springs, take the Central Road to Herkimer, eighty-one miles distant. For Avon Springs, Central Railroad to Rochester; Trenton Falls, Central Road to Utica. Also, for Niagara Falls, Central Railroad direct, three hundred and five miles.

Troy,

Situated at the head of navigation, is one hundred and fifty miles from New York, and a beautiful city of forty-five thousand inhabitants. It lies along the river for about three miles, and drops back a mile from east to west. It is a thriving city, with its large manufacturing interests; also, a great railway centre.

We will now accompany the tourist a little further north, to Saratoga, Lake George, and Lake

To Travellers, Theatre-goers, &c.

BRILLIANT AND POWERFUL DAY AND NIGHT DOUBLE PERSPECTIVE GLASSES,

FOR THE SEA, THEATRE, AND GENERAL OUT-DOOR USE,

Combining portability with extraordinary power and wide field of observation; — objects are distinctly seen from 3 to 10 miles, — and Saturn's rings and the double stars are plainly visible.

To be obtained only at

SEMMONS, Optician.
669½ Broadway, N. Y.

EYE-PRESERVERS AND SPECTACLES.

The advantages of these celebrated glasses over all others are: they give great relief to weak, dim, and defective vision, — exert no heating influence on the eyes, — and without the distressing effect of frequent changes.

Sole Depot,

SEMMONS, Optician,
669½ Broadway, N. Y.

Champlain, observing, as we pass, the more prominent objects of interest.

The ride from Albany or Troy to the Springs is a most agreeable one, as the route crosses and follows the Hudson and Mohawk Rivers, as it passes Waterford, four miles above Troy, and near the Cohoes Falls, and thence continues upon the west bank of the Hudson, eight miles further, to Mechanicsville. It then crosses the canal, passes "Round Lake," and enters

Balston Spa,

Twenty-five miles from Troy. The mineral waters at this place are not so popular as they were formerly, those of Saratoga being generally preferred. Five miles distant is the Long Lake, a beautiful sheet of water, situated in the midst of charming scenery; it is five miles long, and one wide, and abounds with fish. We will now hasten on to

Saratoga Springs.

This is probably the most famous place of summer resort in the United States, frequented by Americans from all sections of the country, and by foreign tourists from all climes. There is nothing remarkable about the topography or the scenery of Saratoga; on the contrary, the place would be uninteresting enough, but for the virtue of its waters and the pleasures of its brilliant society. The health-giving Springs, of which the fame of Saratoga has been born were discovered in 1792, though they were long before known to and considered of value by the Indians. There are eleven Springs in the vicinity of Saratoga. No charge is made for the water, except what visitors voluntarily give those who wait upon them at the Spring. The "chief end of man" at Saratoga is to drink and to dance,—the one in the earliest possible morning, and the other at the latest conceivable night. Among the pleasures outside of Saratoga is a jaunt to Saratoga Lake, six miles away. Here is to be found nice boating, and sometimes "make believe" to fish. The Lake is nine miles long, and about three in width.

A visit to Lake George is a delightful episode and variation in Saratoga life. Let us therefore take the cars to Moreau Station, fifteen miles distant, and thence by stage to

Glen's Falls,

Where we will stop and lunch. This is a pleasant village, nine miles from the Lake. This place is trebly interesting from its natural, its poetical and its historical character. The passage of the Upper Hudson here is through a rude ravine, with a descent of seventy-five feet over a rocky precipice nine hundred feet in length, which may be seen from the bridge in the village. When within three miles of Lake George we pass the storied waters of *Bloody Pond*, and near by is the historic stone called *Williams' Rock*. Near this

BRASS AND ZINC
STAIR PLATES.

IN DIFFERENT PATTERNS OF ANY SHAPE AND SIZE REQUIRED,
FOR STEAMBOATS, HOTELS, PUBLIC BUILDINGS, ETC.

The most ornamental, as well as economical article in the saving of oil-cloth and stairs.

Also,

STAIR RODS

IN EVERY VARIETY OF

BRONZE, FINE GILT and SILVER, with PATENT FASTENINGS.

Balsley's Patent Step-Ladder,

$20 Gold Coin Business Cards,

Upholstery and Trunk Hardware manufactured by

W. T. & J. MERSEREAU,

62 Duane Street,

𝔑𝔢𝔴 𝔜𝔬𝔯𝔨.

Factory, NEWARK, N. J.

WILLIAM H. ELDER

(SUCCESSOR TO JULIUS GARELLY,)

Manufacturer, Importer,

AND

Wholesale Dealer in

LADIES'

Dress and Mantilla

TRIMMINGS,

Gimps, Fringes, Galoons, Braids, Bindings, Buttons, Beltings, &c. &c. &c.

No. 101 Franklin Street,

New York.

rock Colonel Williams was killed in an engagement with the French and Indians, September 8, 1755. The slain (about one thousand) in this unfortunate battle were cast into the waters near by, since called Bloody Pond. It may be passed unnoticed, without being pointed out, as it is surrounded by foliage.

We are now brought, after a delightful ride, to

Lake George,

And stop at Caldwell, a little village at the head of the Lake; one of the most lovely places imaginable to spend the summer season. The Lake House and Fort William Henry Hotel are excellent places: the latter, a new and elegant structure, near the ruins of the old Fort on the right. About a mile southeast are the ruins of Fort George. These localities are seen from the piazza of the hotel, which commands also a fine view of the Lake, with its many islands. The passage of Lake George, thirty-six miles to the landing near the village of Ticonderoga, and four miles from the venerable ruins of Fort Ticonderoga, on Lake Champlain, is very delightful.

We will therefore bid good-by to Caldwell, at the head of the Lake, and proceed on our voyage down one of the handsomest and most delightful waters in the United States. The first object of interest which attracts our attention is Diamond Island. Here, in 1777, was a military depot of Burgoyne's army, and an encounter between the

garrison and a detachment of American troops.
Dome Island is passed in the centre of the Lake,
twelve miles from Caldwell. General Putnam's
army took shelter here while he went to apprise
General Webb of the movements of the enemy
at the mouth of the Northwest bay. About here
is one of the most beautiful parts of Lake George.
Just beyond, on the left, is Bolton, with an inviting
place of sojourn, called the "Mohican House."
Just above, on the east side, is the bold semi-
circular palisades called Shelving Rock. Passing this picturesque feature of the landscape, we
enter the "Narrows" at the base of the boldest
and loftiest shores of Horicon. At this point,
Black Mountain rises, with an altitude of two
thousand two hundred feet. Emerging from the
Narrows on the north, we approach a projecting
strip of land called

Sabbath Day Point,

So named by General Abercrombie, from his
having embarked his army on the spot on a Sunday morning. The place is remembered also as
the scene of a fight in 1775 between the Colonists
and a party of the French and Indians. Again, in
1776, Sabbath Day Point was the scene of a battle
between some Americans and a party of Indians.
As the boat passes the Point and the Summer
Hotel at "Garfield's," Anthony's Nose is seen on
the right, and on the left

THE WOODS AND ATLD TRIBES MOUNTAIN AND THE ON THE CAÑON WALL

WATERS'
First Premium
#

WITH IRON FRAME, OVERSTRUNG BASS AND AGRAFFE BRIDGE.

MELODEONS, PARLOR, CHURCH, & CABINET
ORGANS.

The best Manufactured; Warranted for six years.

100 Pianos, Melodeons, and Organs, of six first-class makers, *at low prices for Cash,* or one-quarter cash and the balance in monthly instalments. Pianos for rent, and rent money applied if purchased. Second-hand instruments at great bargains. Illustrated Catalogues mailed. (*Mr. Waters is the author of six Sunday-School Music Books;* "Heavenly Echoes," and "New S. S. Bell," just issued.)

Warerooms, 481 Broadway, New York.

HORACE WATERS & CO.

TESTIMONIALS.

"The Waters Pianos are known as among the very best." *N. Y. Evangelist.*

"We can speak of the merits of the Waters Pianos from personal knowledge as being of the very best quality."— *Christian Intelligencer.*

"We have one of Mr. Waters' Pianos now in our residence, (where it has stood for years,) of which any manufacturer in the world might well be proud. We have always been delighted with it as a sweet-toned and powerful instrument, and there is no doubt of its durability; more than this, some of the best amateur players in the city, as well as several celebrated pianists, have performed on the said piano, and all pronounce it a superior and first-class instrument. Stronger indorsement we could not give." — *Home Journal.*

Roger's Slide,

A rugged promontory four hundred feet high, with a steep face of bare rock, down which the Indians, to their great bewilderment, supposed the bold Major Rogers to have passed when they pursued him to the brink of the precipice. This pass is very much like that of the Highlands of the Hudson. Two miles beyond is Prisoners' Island, where, during the French war, those captured by the English were confined; and directly west is Lord Howe's Point, where the English army, under Lord Howe, consisting of 16,000 men, landed, previous to the attack on Ticonderoga. We are now approaching the termination of our excursion on this beautiful Lake, and in a mile we reach Ticonderoga, whence stages run a distance of three miles over a romantic road to

Fort Ticonderoga, on Lake Champlain.

This fortification, the ruins of which are visible, was built by the French in 1756. It was a place of much strength; its natural advantages were very great, being surrounded by water on three sides, and having its fourth covered by a swamp, and the only point by which it could be approached by a breastwork. It was afterwards, however, easily reduced by an expedient adopted by General Burgoyne—that of placing artillery on Mount Defiance, on the south side of the Lake George outlet, entirely commanding the fort, from which shot was thrown into the midst of the enemy's works. Fort Ticonderoga was one of the first strongholds taken from the English at the commencement of the Revolutionary war. Colonel Ethan Allen of Vermont, at the head of the Green Mountain Boys, surprised the unsuspecting garrison, proceeded to the bedside of the Commandant and demanded the surrender of the fort. "In whose name, and to whom?" asked the astonished officer. "In the name of the Great Jehovah and the Continental Congress," spoke the intrepid Allen. The fort was immediately surrendered. It was recaptured by the British two years after, and held during the war.

After exploring the interesting ruins of this ancient fort, and dining at the excellent hotel which stands upon the margin of a beautiful lawn, sloping to the Champlain shore, the tourist may here proceed northward by steamboat, and view the many beauties of Lake Champlain,—to Burlington, Vermont, or Rouse's Point, and thence to Montreal, Canada, forty-seven miles distant by rail; or return by boat to Whitehall, at the head of the Lake, and thence to Rutland and the East; or return to Saratoga, by railroad; or, if preferred, return to Caldwell in time for tea.

We have thus far accompanied the tourist over many delightful places, and together enjoyed very many pleasant scenes, but now we must most respectfully part company, and confide to other hands the pleasure-seeker and tourist.

www.ingramcontent.com/pod-product-compliance
Lightning Source LLC
Chambersburg PA
CBHW031741230426
43669CB00007B/433